Upholstery Repair
and Restoration

Upholstery Repair and Restoration

Robert J. McDonald

B T Batsford Limited   London

DEDICATION

To my wife Anne for her patience and understanding whilst writing this book. To my daughter Shirley for her immaculate typing and her husband Roger for allowing me to take so much of her time. Last but not least to my grand-daughter Anita Elizabeth for providing delightfully entertaining interludes between chapters.

My thanks to Jerry Young for his assistance with the photography.

© Robert J. McDonald 1977
First published 1977
Second impression 1978

ISBN 0 7134 0549 X

Filmset in 11 on 12pt Ehrhardt by
Servis Filmsetting Limited, Manchester

Printed in Great Britain by
The Anchor Press Ltd, Tiptree, Essex
for the Publishers **B T Batsford Limited**
4 Fitzhardinge Street, London W1H 0AH

CONTENTS

SECTION ONE

Introduction

THE CRAFT OF UPHOLSTERY

There can be few more satisfying crafts than the craft of upholstery. I have been engaged in the craft ever since leaving school at the age of 14. I started in the trade as 'shop-boy', and progressed through various stages, situations and areas of responsibility to the time of writing this book, and I hope to carry on for many more years.

Whilst my everyday duties at The London College of Furniture keep me desk-bound a good deal of the time, I am never happier than with an upholsterer's hammer in my hand and a good piece of upholstery to work upon. I still find the work satisfying and, indeed, fascinating.

During many a discussion about furniture with colleagues, I have frequently been chided for insisting that the traditional craft of upholstery is more demanding in terms of skill and patience than many other aspects of furniture making. To a degree, one can liken the skill of the upholsterer to that of a sculptor, where materials have to be coaxed into aesthetically pleasing shapes. An eye for the pleasing curve, the perfect scroll and, indeed, for a straight line is absolutely necessary, as is, of course, infinite patience.

It is true to say that over the last 20 to 30 years economic pressures have brought about considerable changes in the upholstery trade, forcing manufacturers to produce more economically with a smaller labour force, particularly for the popular market. This has encouraged the introduction of new methods and materials entirely foreign to traditional trade practices – a development which a number of the old school of craft upholsterers find difficult to accept. Modern upholstery construction uses a wide range of preformed materials and units for assembly on to chair and settee frames. Such assembly work requires a lesser degree of skill than the use of loose fillings and coil springs which are sewn into the item, singly. The K.D. (knock-down) or part assembly frame has become more popular with producers for its ease of transportation.

Many upholsterers trained in modern techniques of construction have had no experience of traditional materials, such as loose hair and fibre fillings and coil springs, etc. Thus, today's 'craftsman' may be capable of dealing with only one type of upholstery.

I hope that this book will give an insight into the techniques of the deeper craft of upholstery, and be of interest to the craftsman who has missed out in this area during his training.

Although a high percentage of present day upholstery is produced with the aid of modern techniques, there is, nevertheless, a sizeable amount of custom-built work. Many clients still choose the highly skilled craft job irrespective of cost. In addition, the large amount of antique and semi-antique upholstery in existence needs refurbishing by highly skilled upholsterers. Unfortunately, when needed for this work, experienced craftsmen are difficult to find because relatively few young people are willing to undertake the long apprenticeship necessary for training. The retiring craft upholsterers are not being replaced in sufficient numbers. Again, I would hope perhaps that this book will encourage a young person enough to want to 'join the ranks'.

Past experience of teaching, and discussions with students learning upholstery techniques, have given me an insight into what is required from a book of this nature. I find many text books omit vital details, and only briefly explain certain processes. In writing this book, I have tried to avoid these faults.

The earlier pages of the book, which describe some elementary work as an introduction to upholstery, give fairly detailed explanations of various fundamental processes which are repeated (with slight modifications) in various styles of work. Once these have been mastered and confidence gained in tackling each different style, the work becomes much simpler. As the book progresses to the more advanced types of upholstery, the processes which frequently re-appear, and which have previously been explained, are mentioned by name only. A smaller section of the book is devoted to the use of modern materials in upholstery. No doubt some readers will have items of this nature which they may wish to re-upholster.

Very seldom is it possible to convert a frame designed for modern techniques to a traditional style and, conversely, a frame designed for traditional upholstery needs considerable conversion to adapt it for the application of modern foams and suspensions to the seat. Readers will probably find obtaining materials for the refurbishing of the modern style of upholstery easier, and certainly more convenient to use, than the traditional materials for the traditional approach. Reference to the cost of materials has been deliberately omitted, as it can be very misleading in a book of this nature particularly some years after publication.

Over the years, a great deal more timber furniture has survived than upholstered furniture owing to the durable nature of 'hard' timber furniture, and the fragile and perishable nature of materials used in upholstered items.

In the past, greater skill was required from the 'upholder' (as he was then called) than now, for the elaborate and highly decorative work he was called upon to perform. In addition to upholstery work, he was responsible for the complete furnishing of houses, being called upon for curtain making and hanging, wall coverings and hangings, beds, bed hangings and floor coverings. A number of upholsterers were until recent times also coffin makers and funeral furnishers. As a craftsman of high status the upholsterer was one of the élite, often sporting a top hat and tail coat. The Worshipful Company of Upholders was one of the earliest guilds of the City of London. It was granted a coat of arms in 1465. Each of the many jobs the upholsterer was in earlier days expected to tackle and master is now carried on in separate establishments by skilled craftsmen who specialize in just the one craft.

The very earliest attempts at upholstery were the squab cushions on chairs, settles and wooden storage chests to relieve the hardness of the seats. First developments in basic upholstered work were X chairs (figure 1) and Knole settees (figure 2), during the period 1610 to 1620. These were said to have been specially made for a visit of James I to Knole House at Sevenoaks in Kent. The framework of X chairs was completely covered in leather or fabric closely nailed with fancy brass nails along the edges of the cross members to hide the joins of the leather or fabric. Seats were thick squabs filled with lambswool or horsehair resting upon straps or fabric stretched and nailed across the seat members. The backs were narrow strips of leather or were very thinly upholstered across the two uprights.

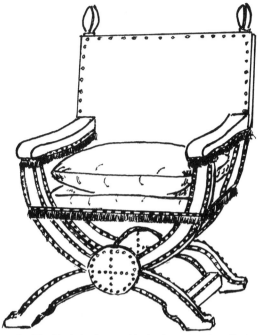

1 *The X chair. Covered in leather, closely nailed.*

The first use of 'stuffover' upholstery came during the reign of Queen Anne, in the early eighteenth century, with framed constructions such as wing chairs, again designed to keep away draughts in the larger livingrooms of the day. All upholstery was 'top' stuffed, and rested on suspensions stretched across the upper edges of the frame rails. Coil springing came into English upholstery some time later, around 1828, being patented by Samuel Pratt. Prior to this, all upholstery was firmly filled with horsehair or lambswool.

Early frame constructions consisted mostly of mortice and tenon joints, dowelling being introduced with the advent of woodworking machinery, although the occasional dowel joint will be found in the earlier work.

Leather as upholstery covering has always enjoyed popularity. Chippendale, Hepplewhite and Sheraton, however, made good use of morocco (goat skin), considered by many to be more refined than cow-hide. The use of morocco for upholstery covering has virtually ceased these days mainly owing to its high cost. Being a smaller skin it involves more wastage, and it also needs greater care in use as a covering.

Haircloth, a cotton weave with real horsehair woven into the weft, was also used during this period. It is now seldom used but is still obtainable. Detachable seats and

Knole settees (which are still very popular even today) were box-like, sparsely upholstered constructions with high backs and high adjustable sides to keep out the draughts whistling across the high, wide, open halls of the day. The Knole settees were heavily decorated across the backs and across the seat squabs with braid containing gold thread. They had deep fringes around the base, and were frequently decorated with pelmets draped down the back.

During the unsettled and troubled times prior to the mid-seventeenth century, comfort in the home was neglected and thought to be effeminate. Most seating was either hard, or with hammock-type suspension. Cane seating with velvet or tapestry-covered cushions was introduced to relieve the hardness and give decoration to chairs and day beds.

The William and Mary period saw the introduction of Indian printed cotton (chintz), petit point embroidery, damasks, brocades and crewel work, with the use of elaborate trimmings.

2 *The Knole settee. Elaborately trimmed.*

backs upholstered as separate pieces for chairs were frequently used, and covered in haircloth. These were designed to allow for finer and more elaborate mouldings around the edges of seats and backs which were too flimsy to attach the upholstery in the conventional way. The elaborate trimmings used earlier were discarded and replaced with finer mouldings, neat narrow gimps or decorative brass nailing.

During the early nineteenth century developments in the textile industry, e.g. the invention of the Jacquard loom in 1803, resulted in newer and less expensive fabrics for upholstery use. With the introduction of coil springing into upholstery in 1828, the aesthetic appearance of upholstered pieces disappeared through the over-use of the spring, resulting in the large Victorian deeply sprung and deeply buttoned couches and chairs which had less of the 'fine craft' appearance.

A large amount of Victorian period upholstery still exists – the more attractive pieces are sought after and command a good price even with the upholstery in poor condition. Many of the Victorian chairs and couches in existence are badly upholstered with badly constructed frameworks. Poor quality fillings were frequently used, such as woodwool (wood shavings) and shoddy (rag flock). The most popular filling of that time was a dried seaweed called alva used as a 'first stuffing', with cotton flock as the final or second filling. There is little point in salvaging any of these fillings – they are virtually 'dead'. Where horsehair has been used in an older piece of upholstery it usually is of a far better quality than is obtainable currently so is worth salvaging.

Any craftsman worth his salt will take pride in gathering a comprehensive range of tools to enable him to ply his trade, to be able to cope with any type of work with which he may be presented. The upholsterer working on hand-made traditional upholstery will need far more tools than one dealing with items using preformed fillings and prefabricated units, geared to speedier mass production methods.

To work as efficiently and comfortably as possible, work should be arranged or positioned at the correct height to avoid backache and strain, particularly during lengthy operations. Very little upholstery work requires the upholsterer to work on his knees at floor level. The ideal support for work, of course, is a pair of trestles of a suitable height to suit the worker (plate 1). A short person will find rather lower trestles more comfortable to work with, whilst the taller person will find trestles with longer legs more convenient. The normal height is 74 cm (2 ft 5 in.) with a top platform of 15 cm (6 in.) width with a fillet nailed around the outer edge to prevent the feet or legs of the work from slipping off the edges of the trestles.

Whilst the trestles will be used for most of the larger work, a number of smaller items the upholsterer is called upon to do will require a flat surface, such as a board which can be laid across the trestles (plate 2). To prevent any movement of the board whilst laid across the trestles, two cross members should be screwed to the underside of the board to locate into the channel on the top platform of the trestles. Both trestles and board may be made from softwood. Provided they are of sound construction, they should last for many years.

Figure 3 illustrates and names the basic tools needed for the average upholstery project. The upholstery craftsman is fortunate in that the kit of tools necessary to ply his trade are fairly inexpensive compared with other skilled craftsmen. A cabinet-

1 Trestle suitable for upholstery work made from soft wood.

2 Smaller articles needing a board laid across trestles.

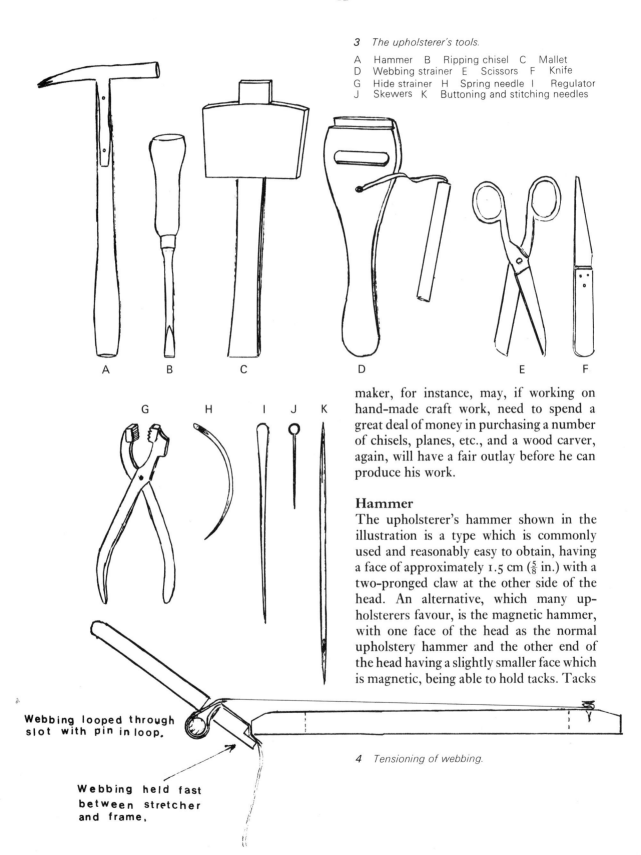

3 The upholsterer's tools.

A Hammer B Ripping chisel C Mallet
D Webbing strainer E Scissors F Knife
G Hide strainer H Spring needle I Regulator
J Skewers K Buttoning and stitching needles

maker, for instance, may, if working on hand-made craft work, need to spend a great deal of money in purchasing a number of chisels, planes, etc., and a wood carver, again, will have a fair outlay before he can produce his work.

Hammer

The upholsterer's hammer shown in the illustration is a type which is commonly used and reasonably easy to obtain, having a face of approximately 1.5 cm ($\frac{5}{8}$ in.) with a two-pronged claw at the other side of the head. An alternative, which many upholsterers favour, is the magnetic hammer, with one face of the head as the normal upholstery hammer and the other end of the head having a slightly smaller face which is magnetic, being able to hold tacks. Tacks

Webbing looped through slot with pin in loop.

Webbing held fast between stretcher and frame.

4 Tensioning of webbing.

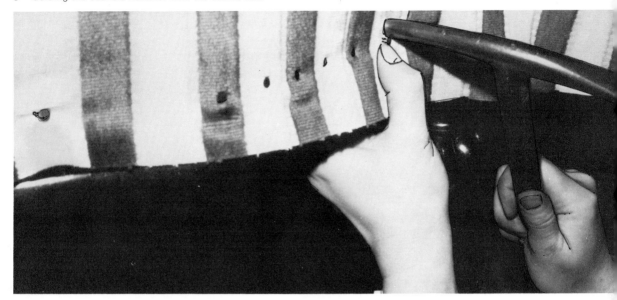

may be positioned on this magnetic face and hammered into the timber without having to press the tack in position with the thumb. The person not used to the magnetic hammer can sometimes find them a little inconvenient as they tend to pick up tacks from the work bench when the hammer is laid upon it.

A further hammer which is a 'must' for the fine craftsman is the cabriole hammer. This should be used when hammering tacks adjacent to rebated polished edges or tacking materials close to carved edges. The cabriole hammer is a lightweight hammer with a smaller face than the usual type (approximately 0.7 cm or 0.8 cm ($\frac{5}{16}$ in.) in diameter). This should always be used when there is a danger of the larger face bruising the polished edges. The thumb nail should be used to guide the hammer onto the tack head (plate 3).

Webbing stretcher

Use of the 'bat' type webbing stretcher is illustrated in figure 4 and plates 4 and 5, but plates 6, 7 and 8 show alternative types of stretchers and the methods of use. It is

possible in an emergency, where the normal tool is not available, to tension webbing with the aid of a piece of flat timber only (plate 9) but is not so convenient or quick as the proper tool.

Ripping chisel

This may be in two forms, with a straight blade, as in the illustration (figure 3b) or a shaped blade. There is no distinct advantage in using one or the other – it is a matter of preference, and of getting accustomed to using a particular type.

Mallet

The normal type of cabinet-maker's mallet, or perhaps a slightly lighter type, will be suitable. It is essential to use a wooden mallet when using a ripping chisel. Remember that any wooden-handled tool should only be struck with another wooden object, not a metal hammer which would quickly split the handle of the ripping chisel.

4   Threading webbing through 'bat'-type stretcher.
5   Tensioning of webbing using 'bat'-type stretcher.
6   Tensioning webbing using 'U' bar stretcher.

7   Using spiked-type stretcher positioning webbing.
8   Tensioning of webbing using the spiked stretcher.
9   Using block of wood to tension webbing.

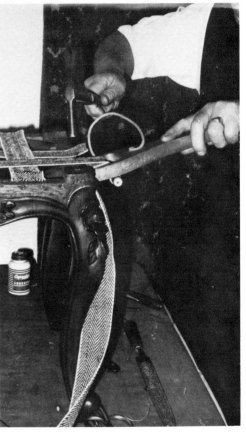

Scissors

It is most important to have a good quality pair of scissors, especially for a professional upholsterer; 20 or 25 cm (8 on 9 in.) are suitable sizes. When purchasing, one should test the fit of the fingers in the loops – for the larger hand the smaller size will be most uncomfortable. The blades of the scissors can be kept keen and sharp if they are carefully honed occasionally with a fine carborundum stone. The stone should be held steady at the correct angle of the existing cutting edge and rubbed along the blade five or six times (plate 10).

Hide strainers

Similar to a pair of pliers but with wide jaws, approximately 6 cm (2½ in.) wide. Intended to assist with the tensioning of leather used on upholstery work. These can also be used for the re-tensioning of webbing where the original webbing is lifted at one end to be restretched and re-tacked. Having short ends of webbing, the normal 'bat' type of stretcher cannot be used.

Leather cutting knife

Similar to shoe-repairer's knife – can be kept sharpened with the use of a fine carborundum stone.

Regulator

A flat-ended pointed instrument available in various sizes from 15 cm to 30 cm (6 to 12 in.). Used for 'regulating' fillings, the flat end being useful for smoothing and setting pleating, particularly in deep buttoning.

Needles

A number of different sizes and types of needles will be required. Spring needle – a fairly strong curved needle for inserting 'bridle' ties, twine loops into hessian to hold fillings in place, sewing in springs and a number of other tasks. Large and small circular needles – 15 cm (6 in.) large and 7.5 cm (3 in.) small. Bayonet needles for stitching and fine needles for buttoning, the bayonet needles having a triangular point whilst buttoning needles are smooth throughout their length.

Skewers

Long pins with a ringed end 7.5 or 10 cm (3 or 4 in.) in length used for holding materials temporarily in position before fixing or tacking permanently. Also for sprung edge work, having many other uses.

Other tools

Further tools will be needed from time to time, such as a wood rasp, cabinet hammer, pair of pincers, pair of dividers (for spacing of decorative nails), etc. However, these are not strictly upholstery tools.

MATERIALS

Upholstered work is constructed from a fairly wide range of commodities often in varying grades or qualities, some being suitable for specific operations and others not. It is part of the craft to gain a thorough knowledge of this aspect of the work, together with the uses, advantages or disadvantages of each item.

Some difficulty may be experienced in obtaining small quantities of materials for the odd repair, but there are a number of suppliers now prepared to offer upholstery sundries in small lots by postal service.

Since most commodities are supplied in various grades or qualities, their costs vary considerably. It is not always prudent to opt for the cheaper grade; as a general rule, the higher outlay for the better grade is a good investment. Upholstery using the poorest quality materials will have a comparatively short life. It is pointless to produce work with a high labour and skill content which will need re-upholstery within a short time because the materials have worn out. This also applies to covering fabrics; the cheaper types do generally soil and wear more quickly than their better counterparts.

Tacks

A wide range of different size tacks are used in traditional upholstery. Whilst it is not strictly necessary to have the complete range to hand whilst working, it is important to have as wide a selection as possible so the correct tack may be selected for a particular operation. It is difficult to lay down any hard and fast rules regarding the use of tacks; it is more a case of learning from experience. As a general rule, the tack should be small enough not to split the timber and large enough to hold the particular material successfully without any danger of pulling away. For example, when applying linen webbing to the base of an easy chair seat, as the timber is normally of a heavy section, a 1.6 cm ($\frac{5}{8}$ in.) tack may be successfully used, preferably the improved type which has the larger head to hold the webbing securely in position. Should the webbing operation be carried out on a light loose seat frame, or another type of frame with thinner section timber, a 1.2 cm ($\frac{1}{2}$ in.) improved tack would be more appropriate. Alternatively, if the timber is particularly hard (as sometimes it may be) a 1.2 cm ($\frac{1}{2}$ in.) fine tack would be the better choice because being thinner this would enter the harder timber more easily with less risk of damaging the frame through heavy hammering to drive the tack home.

Very short 0.7 cm ($\frac{1}{4}$ in.) tacks are used only for tacking fabric to thin plywood facings or hardboard, etc. They are not normally used for the general run of upholstery work.

'Gimp' pins, thin tacks lacquered black or in many colours, are useful to have to hand. Used for applying gimp or securing covering where the normal tack would look unsightly, a black or coloured gimp pin will often blend with the covering material and not be visible.

Tack sizes available:
    1.6 cm ($\frac{5}{8}$ in.) improved
    1.6 cm ($\frac{5}{8}$ in.) fine

1.2 cm ($\frac{1}{2}$ in.) improved
1.2 cm ($\frac{1}{2}$ in.) fine
1.0 cm ($\frac{3}{8}$ in.) improved
1.0 cm ($\frac{3}{8}$ in.) fine
1.2 cm ($\frac{1}{2}$ in.) gimp pins
1.0 cm ($\frac{3}{8}$ in.) gimp pins

All tacks, other than gimp pins, are supplied as 'improved' or 'fine'. These are terms used to describe the thickness of the shank and size of the head of the tack. 'Improved' tacks will have a thicker shank and larger head than their 'fine' counterparts. Tacks are normally supplied in packets of $\frac{1}{2}$ kilo or $\frac{1}{2}$ lb or in larger quantity bags for the professional. 'Blued' cut tacks usually are the better buy, having sharper points.

Staples

When attempts are made to re-cover contemporary furniture, staples are often found holding the covering, etc. These are sometimes very difficult to remove. Pointed staple removers are obtainable but do not always work very well. The normal upholsterer's regulator will remove staples as well as any patented device. By easing the point of the regulator under the crown of the staple it can be easily levered up, and the use of a pair of pincers after the crowns have been raised will make short work of their removal.

Professional upholsterers working on modern constructions mostly use staples fired into the timber with the aid of compressed air, working with a pressure of 80 to 100 lbs per sq. in. (plates 11 and 12). The electric staple gun is a more portable tool needing only a power socket to plug into. Both guns are fairly expensive tools, the air gun needing an air compressor which can operate many guns simultaneously, with the air having piped outlets to the working stations. Neither of these guns is economic for the small upholstery operator. Should stapling be required, perhaps for upholstery mounted on plywood, a manual hand gun can be used, being relatively cheap to buy and supply with staples (plate 13). The size of staples normally used are 1.2 cm ($\frac{1}{2}$ in.) crown (width) with either 0.6 cm or 1 cm ($\frac{1}{4}$ in. or $\frac{3}{8}$ in.) leg.

11 Compressed-air staple gun.

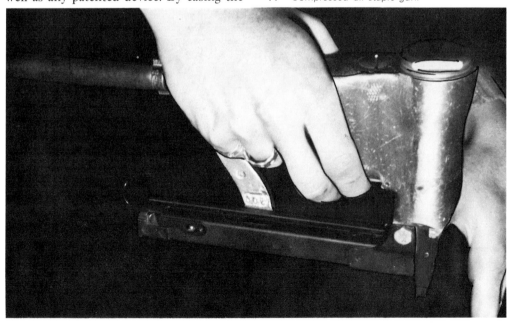

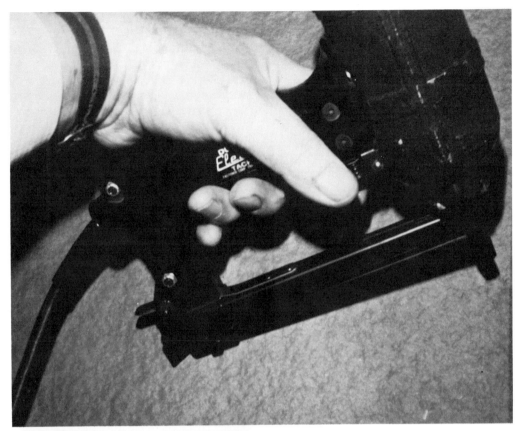

12 Electric staple gun.

13 Hand-operated gun.

Webbing

Webbing used for traditional upholstery work varies from 4.5 cm (1¾ in.) to 9 cm (3½ in.), 5 cm (2 in.) being the most generally used. 'English' herringbone twill weave (black and white) is regarded as best. Flax and cotton fibre, used in the making of the best webbing, is costly, but will last many years and will stretch very little. The better quality jute webbing can be reliable provided a good grade is used. The grading of webbing is by weight per gross yards. The black and white herringbone type is usually supplied in rolls of 18 metres or yards; jute in rolls of 36 metres or yards.

Hessian

This is woven from fibres from the stem of the jute plant, and supplied in many qualities, graded by weight per yard × 40 in. Whenever possible, the best quality should be used, particularly over springs. Upholsterers' tarpaulin hessian with a double warp yarn should be used for work where durability rather than cost is the major consideration.

Scrim

A more openly woven material than hessian, better quality scrim is made from fine flax yarn. It is used solely for encasing fibre or hair in the 'first' stuffing of traditional upholstery prior to stitching the edges.

Calico

This is a plainly woven unbleached cotton fabric obtainable in various qualities, used as an undercovering for traditional upholstery. Whilst it is not imperative that an undercovering of calico be used in all cases, it is an advantage to be able to mould fillings into shape with calico prior to applying the top covering fabric, particularly when using fragile or difficult covers or leather.

Cambric

A closely-woven waxed cotton material used in the making of interior cases for feather or down cushions. The waxed surface, which has a slight gloss, should be used as the interior side; it assists in preventing the escape of feathers through the weave.

FILLINGS

Curled hair

This is by far the best type of loose filling but owing to price rises in recent years has, to a certain extent, been ousted by cheaper forms of fillings.

The best grades of hair are from horse manes and tails and from the tails of cattle, these being very long stranded. A lower grade hair is obtained from the hog; this is much shorter than horse hair and more brittle. Intermediate qualities (hair mixtures) are made by intermixing various percentages of long and short hair. The curl is obtained by tightly twisting the hair into long ropes, steaming and slowly drying to set the curl.

Curled hair is generally used as a 'second' stuffing, that is, over a basic filling of a cheaper, coarser fibre normally put into the 'first' stuffing. In the higher grades of upholstery, where cost is a less important factor, hair will in some instances be used in the first stuffing, in place of the cheaper fibre.

To test the quality of hair, a small quantity of it should be held between the fingers of the two hands and pulled apart. This will show how much of the hair is long stranded, the shorter hogs' hair will tend to drop away as the long strands separate.

Fibres

Fibres are used only as a 'first' stuffing in upholstered work to obtain the basic shape, a covering of scrim being laid over, tacked and stitched into the required shape.

Two types of fibre are commonly used, coir, which is the ginger-coloured outer covering fibre of the coconut; and Algerian palm grass fibre which has been shredded and dyed black for sterilization against a particular mite. Of the two, Algerian has the better resilience and durability because it is processed in a similar fashion to hair being twisted into rope form to attain a curl in the fibre. This gives it greater bulk and springiness.

Alva
A type of seaweed, not now in commercial use as a filling, alva was often used in the 'first' stuffing of Victorian upholstery. Very similar in appearance to a coarse tobacco, it is not suitable for re-use.

Cotton flock
A 'dated' filling, cotton flock was used extensively in Victorian upholstery in conjunction with alva as a 'second' or top filling. Having very little resilience and tending to flatten quickly, it is not suitable for re-use. An amount of seek husk particles are often found amongst the cotton fibres.

Shoddy (rag flock)
This is a lower grade of filling, sometimes used in upholstery, and manufactured by reducing waste wool or cotton textiles to their original fibre form after a thorough sterilization process, wool flock being more resilient than its cotton counterpart. Currently it is used more as a 'layered' filling.

Kapok
Used mainly as a filling for cushions and some eiderdowns, kapok is a very fine vegetable fibre from the long seed pod from the kapok tree. It has the disadvantage of 'matting' or fusing into balls of fibre after a period of use, but is used in some upholstery in the form of a 'quilt' encased in muslin gauze with long stitches through holding the kapok fibres in position.

Linter felt
A thick 'lap' of cotton fibres frequently used in mass production upholstery laid over other types of loose fillings immediately under the top covering. Generally not suitable for re-use because of its soiled and flattened condition. Supplied by weight in large rolls of approximately 12 metres (13 yards).

Cotton wadding
This is a padding in thin sheet form which acts as an insulation between the filling and top covering. It is supplied in small rolls often with a skin on one surface, and is referred to as 'skin wadding'. The skin should be applied immediately over the filling with the softer side uppermost. At least two layers of wadding should be used, three if of a poor quality. Alternatively, there is non-skin wadding which is thicker and needs to be split to a suitable thickness. This is generally more expensive.

Down
This consists of the light fluffy filaments without any quill shafts from the undercoating of water fowl (duck, goose, swan and eider duck). Generally mixed with water fowl or poultry feathers.

Feathers
These can either be duck, goose, water fowl, or poultry feathers, or mixtures of each, poultry feathers being the poorer quality.

Varying grades of feather and down mixtures can be obtained. Larger percentages of down are included in the costlier product. It must be emphasized that there is a great deal of difference in resilience between feathers and down; feathers tend to be flatter and heavier with hard and often sharp quills, and, when used in a cushion, need to be shaken frequently to retain the plumpness in the cushion.

Layered fillings

A number of fillings are used in 'layered' or preformed shapes. In modern upholstery manufacture this speeds production and ensures that the depth of filling is constant where a number of identical pieces are being produced.

One of the problems in the use of loose fillings is gauging the correct, or suitable, depth of filling to use. One upholsterer could well use perhaps more, or less, than a colleague working alongside. The use of layered fillings produced in a constant thickness sheet form obviates this tendency.

The following fillings are used in layered form: rubberized hair/fibre; interlaced fibre pads; linter felt; woollen felt; latex foam; polyurethane foam; and polyester fibre fill.

The most useful of these, and probably the easiest for the learner to use, are urethane foam (plastic), latex foam (rubber) and rubberized hair (hair mixture and rubber), each of which will enable the professional finish to be obtained reasonably easily.

Alternative fillings

Since most of the warehouses supplying the basic commodities used for upholstery will not deal with the amateur needing supplies in small lots, it is useful to know where to obtain substitutes or alternatives to the more traditional materials and fillings.

One substitute for the 'first' stuffing fibre (coconut or Algerian) is nylon fibre waste, as supplied for the filling of the larger toys or replicas of animals. This material is fairly easily obtained, being supplied in small or large bags from the suppliers of toy making sundries. The waste nylon fibres are fairly coarse, somewhat similar to coir or coconut fibre but longer; these should be 'teased' (opened so the fibres are not matted together). This will give the fibre more resilience and softness, and it can then be worked similar to the normal upholstery filling.

Another substitute is fine stranded wood wool, which is used frequently in the packing and insulating of crockery. This is often available in quantity after a delivery of crockery from the manufacturer to the retailers, who are often glad to dispose of it. Finely shredded wood wool was extensively used as a filling in some types of upholstery some years ago. Its use currently is usually confined to the filling of pouffes. The wood fibres need packing together rather more firmly than normal fibre to prevent too much movement in the fibre; this tends to break the fibre strands if too loose. This type of filling may be covered in scrim and stitched as normal fibre.

The 'second' stuffing of horsehair may be substituted by the polyester fibre Dacron, either loose or in sheet form 68 cm (27 in.) wide, this being laid smoothly over the 'first' stuffing. This polyester fibre (also mentioned in the section on cushion making) is a crimped fibre with a great deal of 'loft' (thickness and resiliency); it can frequently be bought from D.I.Y. stores or markets. Courtelle fibre is very similar and may be used in a similar fashion. It is advisable if using either of these to cover in calico before applying the top covering, thus ensuring the fibre keeps in place. Kapok quilted sheet will also serve as a substitute for horsehair, being laid over the 'first' stuffing scrim. This is available from a number of sources.

Many refurbishing jobs on easy chairs and settees may utilise latex or urethane foams, either replacing the horsehair over the 'first' filling, or completely replacing all the fillings using suitable thicknesses of foam. Sheet foam is normally available in a number of thicknesses from 6 mm ($\frac{1}{4}$ in.) to 100 mm (4 in.). This is the normal cushion thickness. When using foam in this way, it is advisable to cut templates from stout paper or fabric to the size and shape of the piece needed. This will avoid wastage in cutting. The foam should be fixed into its position in a similar way to the foam on the stools, having calico or fabric strips stuck to the foam which can then be tacked into position on the frame.

TERMS AND PROCESSES

Back-tacking

This is a method of tacking sections of covering, e.g., outside arms, outside backs, borders, etc., so that the tacking line is not visible. The top edge of the covering is tacked with the reverse side of the material uppermost on the top rail (figure 5). The tacking line should be reinforced with a strip of card, hessian or webbing to achieve a firm straight line. The covering is then laid over so that the back-tacking line is hidden and tacked off on the underside of the frame. It is not practical to back-tack shaped lines due to the weave of the fabric being thrown out of straight.

Pull-over edge

Plate 14 shows an edge which is finished perpendicular with the base rail. The covering is 'pulled over' in one piece from the seat surface to the underside or front edge of the base rail.

Under-the-edge

This is generally used where a front border is needed to cover a depth of springing, such as on the front of cushion seats. A roll is made on the top edge of the front of the seat, and the seat covering is finished and sewn or tacked to the underside of the roll. A border is then pinned out and sewn or back-tacked immediately under the roll, with piping or decorative upholstery cord to hide the join (figure 6). A similar treatment can be given to back edges also.

Bible front

This finish to the front of a seat enables the depth of the seat (from front to back) to be upholstered deeper than the front base rail (figure 7). It can be formed by making a large stitched roll on the cane of a sprung edge, taking the filling and scrim over the cane and stitching through with the cane in the roll, or with a large tack roll on a firm edge.

5 Back-tacking. Outside arm covering back-tacked along side of arm rail.

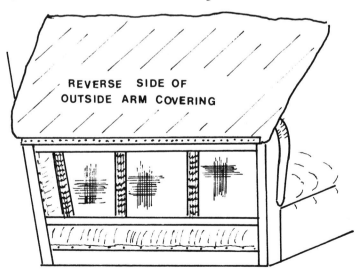

REVERSE SIDE OF
OUTSIDE ARM COVERING

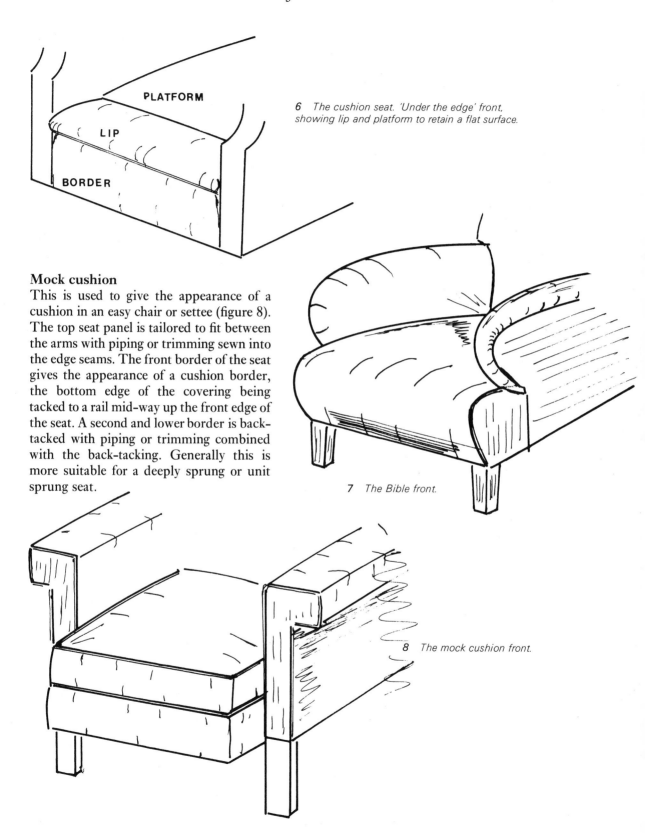

PLATFORM

LIP

BORDER

6 The cushion seat. 'Under the edge' front, showing lip and platform to retain a flat surface.

Mock cushion

This is used to give the appearance of a cushion in an easy chair or settee (figure 8). The top seat panel is tailored to fit between the arms with piping or trimming sewn into the edge seams. The front border of the seat gives the appearance of a cushion border, the bottom edge of the covering being tacked to a rail mid-way up the front edge of the seat. A second and lower border is back-tacked with piping or trimming combined with the back-tacking. Generally this is more suitable for a deeply sprung or unit sprung seat.

7 The Bible front.

8 The mock cushion front.

14 'Pull-over' edge to seat of tub chair.

Lip

Where it is intended to upholster a seat to accommodate a deep bordered cushion, the upper surface of the seat should be made as flat as possible to allow the cushion to lie flat along the front of the edge. In addition to using the filling sparingly to achieve a flat surface, the seat covering should have a tape line or strip of fabric sewn across to form a 'lip' (see figure 6 on page 25). The tape line is stitched through the seat filling with twine approximately 12 to 14 cm (5 to 5½ in.) back from the front edge, pulled up tight to sink the tape line into the filling. Whilst running the twine through the seat with a long needle, the coils of the springs should be avoided with the twine, the spring hessian only should be caught with the twine.

Platform

This describes the part of the seat behind the lip formed for the cushion seat (figure 6 on page 25). The platform on which the cushion rests should be as flat as possible over the surface. Care should be taken not to pull down the sides and back of the platform, this frequently happens whilst tensioning the platform covering, if the seat springing is correct a little slackness in the platform covering is acceptable.

To economize on fabric, the platform covering can be of a lining material similar in colour to the covering material. The platform lining may be machined to the covering fabric used for the lip, in this case the seam between the two materials may be used to run the twine through, so the tape line may be omitted.

Slip-stitching

This is used to close joins between sections of the covering which have been impossible to machine sew beforehand off the job. A small, fine, circular needle, approximately 7.5 cm (3½ in.) is suitable for use with waxed carpet thread or other strong thread (plate 15). Waxed thread is preferable as this is less likely to tangle if one is unused to the operation. Also, it has a longer life, the wax acting as a preservative.

Outside arms, backs, etc., may be back-tacked along their top edges, the lower edge tacked on to the underside of the frame, and the side edges slip-stitched. The stitches should be kept short using, if possible, the same coloured thread as the covering, although, if done correctly, the stitches should not be visible. The circular needle should carry the thread through each piece of covering alternately, the secret of the perfect stitching is to step back fractionally with each stitch as illustrated in figure 9, and to strain the thread tight with each two or three stitches.

Tack roll

This is formed along the edges of seats or backs to provide a soft edge as a quicker, less expensive alternative to stuffing and stitching with fibre and scrim (plates 16, 17, 18). Strips of hessian are tacked using 1.2 cm (½ in.) improved tacks along the rasped edge, so that the tacked edge of hessian will be on the inner part of the roll. After the hessian is tacked in position, the filling is teased and spread evenly along the edge in a similar operation to that of rolling a cigarette. The hessian is then taken over the filling, and tucked under until the required size of roll is obtained; 1.2 cm (½ in.) improved tacks are used to tack the hessian down where it folds under into the roll. The success of making a tack-roll lies in keeping the hessian stretched tightly along its length to ensure that the filling is as even as possible.

At corners the join in the rolls should be mitred, the hessian should be taken over the protruding filling where there are bare ends. The roll should slightly protrude over the face edge of the timber frame, a normal roll would be about 'thumb' size.

15 'Slip' stitching of an outside back.

16 The tack roll. Hessian tacked on rasped edge to contain filling for tack roll. Left-hand side roll completed.

9 Slip-stitching.

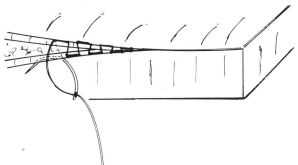

17 'Rolling' hessian over with a filling of fibre to form 'tack-roll'.

18 Typical use of tack roll on front edge of easy chair seat.

Squab

This is a firmly stuffed seat cushion, usually with a narrow border, but occasionally having a 'feather' edge without a border (plate 19). Traditionally it is used on solid wood or cane seats or backs, the squab is made with an inside hair filled case, mattress stitched (a running line stitch) around the edges to keep them firm, ties being inserted at intervals through the top and bottom panels to ensure a flat appearance. Buttons can be used also as an aid to flatness, and also for decoration. The modern counterpart of the squab uses latex or urethane foam.

Skivering

When cutting and preparing leather welting for use in seaming leather sections of the covering, it is more economical to use reasonably short off-cuts instead of cutting long leather strips. Leather welting should be cut 2.8 cm (1⅛ in.) wide in short strips of about 30 cm (12 in.). The face surface of one end should be chamfered away for approximately 1 cm (⅜ in.), and the piece which is to be joined to this should have the under surface chamfered away the same amount so that one will lay upon the other without any visible increase in thickness. The two chamfered or skivered faces should be stuck together with a good adhesive.

A further use of skivering is to shave a thin wafer off the surface of a piece of spare leather which can be stuck over a small flaw or a mark on a finished piece of leather-covered upholstery.

19 Interior of a hair-filled squab cushion made with a hessian case.

Slip-knot

The slip-knot (figure 10) is a quickly made, simple but useful knot, which can be used in many ways when working with twine. It may be used for tying down buttons, but it is essential that the twine twists forming the knot are tight before being slipped down to avoid subsequent slippage or loosening.

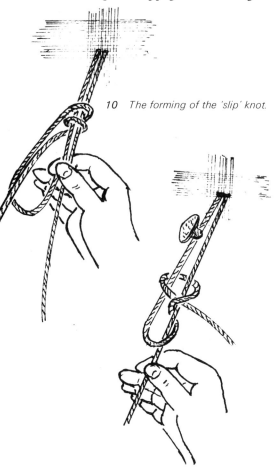

10   The forming of the 'slip' knot.

11   The upholsterer's buttoning knot.

Upholsterer's buttoning knot

This is a slightly more complicated type of slip-knot generally used by the professional for tying down buttons in deeply buttoned work. Once this knot has been pulled down tight it is impossible for it to slip back to release the button (figure 11).

Tack ties

This term is used to indicate a fault in applying the covering to the upholstery (plate 20).

A tack tie is a plainly visible tension line running from the position of a tack which has been hammered in, towards the centre of the covering. This indicates that the covering has been stretched too tightly at that position. This fault is frequently encountered when finely woven fabrics, such as silks, satins and damasks, are applied to panelled backs, pin-stuffed upholstery and the like. To prevent tack ties, the material should be tensioned towards the ends of the tacking lines as well as towards the tacking point (figure 12).

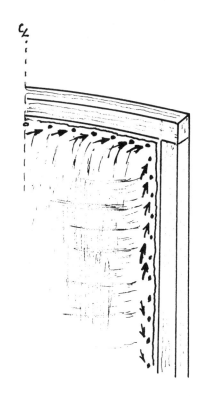

12   Tensioning of fabric to eliminate 'tack ties'.

Collar

This is used to enable the covering to be cut, and to fit snugly around an obstruction without the cut being visible, or the filling working out from under the covering. The collar is used particularly on backs where arm and back meet (figure 13). The back is cut fairly tightly to the contour of the back of the arm, and a strip of fabric is then machined to the contour cut from the back. When the back covering is applied, the machined strip fits tightly like a collar around the arm. This device can also be used in other situations.

Stiles

One of the most difficult areas of upholstery for the learner to understand and master is the cutting of stiles to avoid rails and other obstacles encountered in all but the simplest upholstery work. The cut will vary, according to the shape of the stile and its relationship.

A badly cut stile will eventually allow the filling to work through between timber frame and covering. Compression of the filling causes the covering to be strained away from the stile, and, if not held securely and tensioned correctly the fabric will probably tear, showing frayed ends of yarn. The ideal cut allows the fabric to be tensioned tightly around the stile with a suitable amount of tuck-away material to tack to the frame.

A sharp pair of scissors which comfortably fits the hand are the first requirement for successful cutting. The pair of scissors shown in figure 3 on page 12 have one blade with a sharp point and the other with a flatter end. It is often convenient to use the

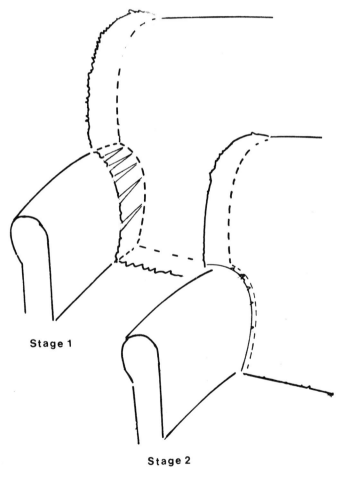

Stage 1

Stage 2

13 *Cutting and fitting a collar. Cover is first temporarily tacked on back and then removed.*

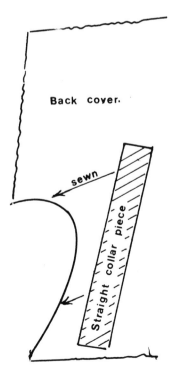

Back cover.

sewn

Straight collar piece

Stage 3

flatter end as the lower blade when cutting, to avoid catching any material on which the scissors are resting whilst being used. Each cut should be clean using the full length of the blades, rather than a series of short snips which leave jagged edges.

Plate 21 shows a seat covering being cut to fit around a back leg of a small chair, a similar cut being needed for the other leg on the left side. The cut is almost completed, the point of the scissors being approximately 0.5 cm ($\frac{1}{4}$ in.) away from the inner corner of the leg.

Prior to the cut being made the covering was folded back squarely and smoothly with the edges of the folded piece parallel with the weave of the fabric. The cut was then made from the extreme corner with the scissors directed to the inner corner of the leg. When the fabric is smoothed back over the side and back it will have sufficient material to tuck in between the stuffing and the frame; the flat end of a regulator is useful for this purpose.

14   Wing chair back cover. Dotted lines show cuts on back cover.

To avoid errors when cutting stiles two golden rules apply: first, the stile should be studied and a suitable method of cutting worked out before the cut is attempted; secondly, it is far better to under cut than to over cut – if at all doubtful do not attempt to cut to the maximum. It is easy to tack the material temporarily while evaluating the cut you have made. If necessary, the covering can then be lifted, and the cut extended. Once a stile has been over cut, rectifying it, if possible at all, will usually pull the weave of the covering out of line. Figures 14 to 17 show other types of cuts which are frequently used in covering upholstery. Figure 18 illustrates how bias piping should be cut.

15   Tub chair seat. Cutting narrow and wide stiles.

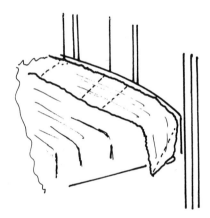

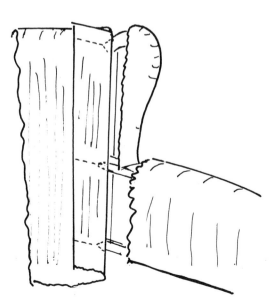

20 Example of tack ties on an outside back of an easy chair covered in a fine silk covering.

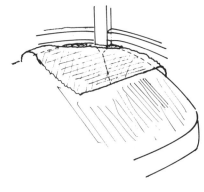

16 *Angled stile cut.*

17 *Arm stile cuts on fireside seat and back.*

18 *Cutting of bias piping, necessary on shaped work.*

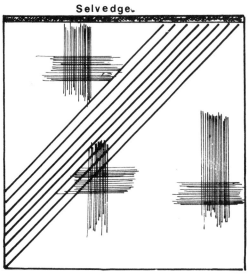

21 Cutting a corner stile of a small chair.

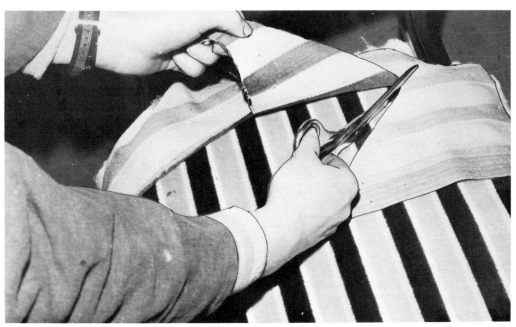

SECTION TWO

Simple Upholstery

UPHOLSTERING A 'DROP IN' SEAT

One of the simplest upholstered pieces for the learner to attempt is the 'drop in' loose seat for a dining or occasional chair. As with most upholstered work, construction can vary according to the outlay and the amount of labour one is prepared to expend. Some variations in the construction of this type of seat are shown in figures 19, 20 and 21. Traditional and contemporary styles are illustrated.

To produce a comfortable and durable job the traditional approach is preferable (figure 22). This, of course, requires a little more time, a more expensive filling and greater expertise in the manipulation of materials to attain the perfect finish, but can be an excellent introduction to upholstery work for the learner.

Preparation

To re-upholster a 'drop in' seat it is usually necessary to strip off all the old upholstery using the ripping chisel (shown in figure 3 on page 12) with the grain of the timber to prevent damage to the frame, particularly at the corners. In some cases it may be found that plywood has been used as a base to support the filling instead of linen or jute webbing. This plywood may be removed if desired and be replaced with webbing to make a more resilient base.

Once the seat frame (usually beech), has been stripped, the top outer edges of the four sides should be chamfered (figure 23). This will allow the filling to be taken to the extreme edges of the frame and prevent any hardness being felt through the final covering.

Before the seat frame is upholstered it should be 'fitted' to accommodate the new covering fabric. A 'drop in' seat should fit comfortably into the rebate of the polished

19, 20, 21 Variations in the construction of loose seats.

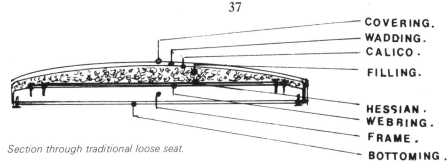

COVERING.
WADDING.
CALICO.
FILLING.

HESSIAN.
WEBBING.
FRAME.
BOTTOMING.

22 Section through traditional loose seat.

base frame. Upholstery fabrics, P.V.C.s and leathers vary in thickness. Should the material used be thicker than the rebated allowance, the finished seat frame will not fit. If then forced or hammered into position, it will cause the polished frame joints to open, resulting in major damage.

A simple method of testing the fit of the seat frame before upholstering it is to place a double thickness of the fabric to be used (over the rebated frame (plate 22), then ease the loose seat frame into position with the doubled fabric between the two frames. With gentle pressure the seat frame should, if the correct size, rest on to the base flange of the rebate. Testing the double thickness on one side is equal to a single thickness each side, but saves effort and time. If the seat is too tight a fit to slide easily into the rebate,

the offending edges should be taken down slightly either with a plane or with a wood rasp, the square face edge of the frame being carefully retained. It is advisable to mark the edge of the frame with pencil to indicate how much needs to be taken off. If there is so much clearance between seat frame and base as to leave an unsightly gap between the upholstered seat and the polished frame, one or two strips of cardboard can be cut to the width of the seat frame edge and tacked along this with 1 cm ($\frac{3}{8}$ in.) fine tacks.

23 Top outer edges of frame should be chamfered.

Top outer edges of frame should be chamfered.

Tensioning the webbing

The method of tensioning the webbing is illustrated in figure 4 and plates 4 to 9. For sound, durable work one should use a good quality webbing. The number of strands of webbing to use will vary, depending upon the size and shape of seat and the open area to be supported. Two strands each way should be the minimum. This is a suitable arrangement for the smaller seat, and often found where economies in cost are being made. Three by two strands of webbing are suitable for the average seat. Strands of webbing must be interlaced alternately to ensure each strand will help to support its neighbour (figure 24). The majority of 'drop in' seats taper from front to back, so webbing applied front to back should also be tapered inwards, although it need not be at such an angle as the timber sides.

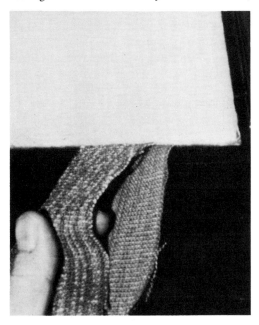

22 Fitting of a loose seat into the polished rebated frame.

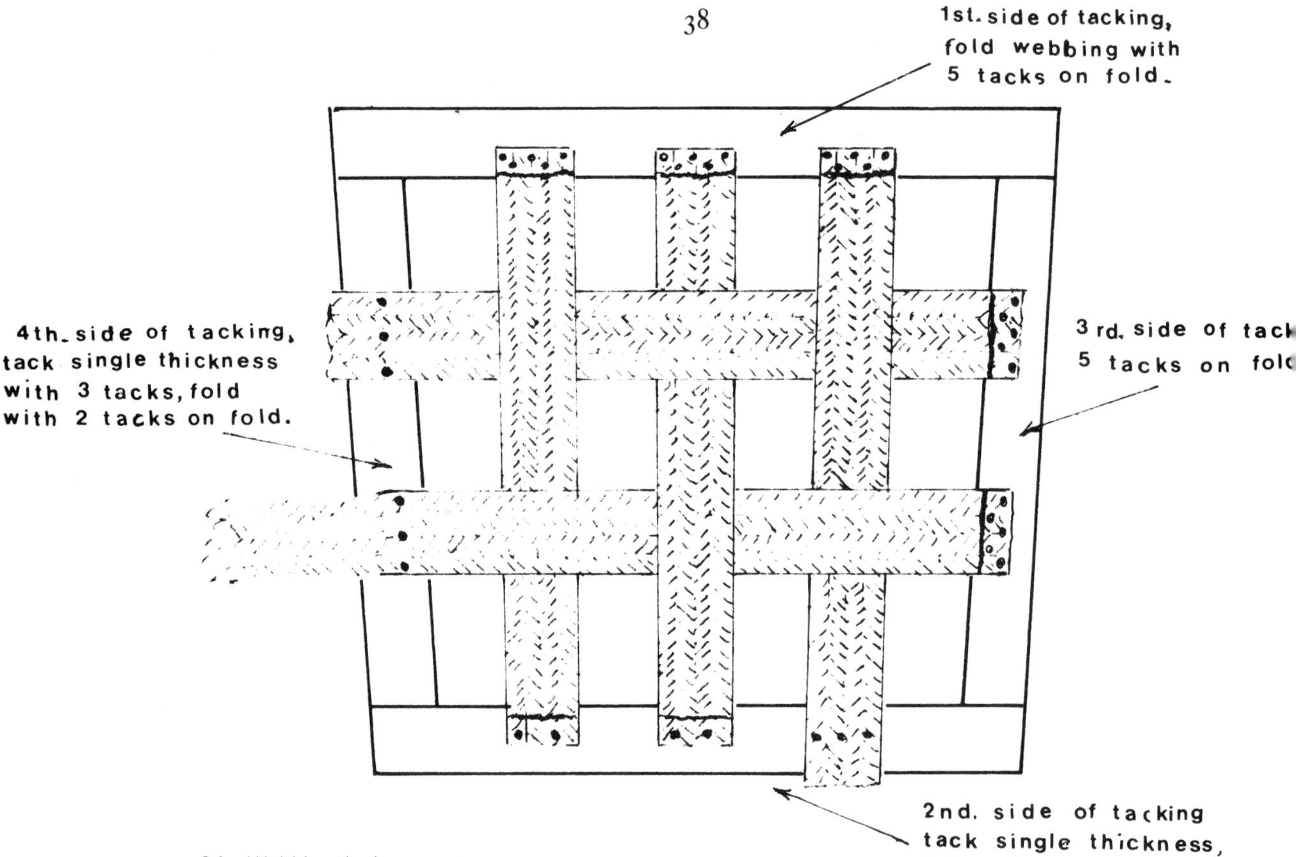

1st. side of tacking,
fold webbing with
5 tacks on fold.

4th. side of tacking,
tack single thickness
with 3 tacks, fold
with 2 tacks on fold.

3rd. side of tack
5 tacks on fold

24   *Webbing the loose seat.*

2nd. side of tacking
tack single thickness,
fold with 2 tacks on fold.

Care should be taken to space the strands of webbing evenly so that the gaps are equal including those between the side webs and the frame. 1.2 cm (½ in.) improved tacks should be used for tacking webbing or, if the timber is particularly hard (as occasionally it is), fine instead of improved tacks may be used. These will not be so difficult to hammer home; also there will be less risk of split timber.

Webbing must be tacked on to the frame under tension but a great deal of care should be used in doing this. In using the 'bat' strainer, it is very easy to ruin a seat or chair frame by over-tensioning. A small, lightly constructed, loose seat frame is particularly vulnerable to this overstraining damage. Such a frame will easily twist. Consequently, when upholstery is complete and the seat applied to the base frame, it will not

sit flat into the rebate. Further damage may also be caused by overstraining to the tacking positions and the yarn forming the weave, particularly with the lower grades of webbing. A good guide for correctly tensioning the webbing is, whilst levering the strainer downwards, to tap the strand of web being tensioned with the side of the hammer head: if too slack the hammer will have a 'dead' bounce, but as the tension is increased so the bounce will become livelier, and once this lively bounce has been achieved the webbing should be tacked off with three tacks, no further straining being necessary.

Applying the hessian

Hessian should now be applied taut over the webbing, tacking with 1 cm ($\frac{3}{8}$ in.) improved tacks. Working with the back of the seat nearest to you, tack the hessian to the front of the seat frame with a fold of approximately 1 cm ($\frac{3}{8}$ in.), and space tacks out approximately 6 cm ($1\frac{1}{4}$ in.) apart. The folded hessian should be tacked just overlapping the webbing which should have been tacked half way across the width of the timber frame.

Now tack the hessian to the back of the frame (the side nearest to you). Put a tack in the centre, and straining the hessian by hand (a tool is not necessary), work progressively towards each corner, inserting the tacks approximately 6 cm ($1\frac{1}{4}$ in.) apart as before. Having tacked the hessian to the front and back of the frame, continue tacking down one side, then tension the hessian across to the remaining side. Remember, it is permissible to tack the first side (front) of hessian with a fold, the remaining three sides should be tacked singly so they may be tensioned. It is difficult to get a good taut surface if you attempt to strain and fold at the same time. Trim off the surplus hessian leaving sufficient to make a fold similar to the fold along the front, then fold over and tack the folded hessian down using the same size tacks with slightly wider spacing.

Inserting the bridle ties

Twine bridle ties should now be sewn into the surface of the hessian (figure 25) using a spring needle. The loops formed should be sufficiently slack to allow the filling to be tucked under, without tearing the hessian or breaking the twine. The twine should be sewn into the hessian as a running line without knotting, other than at the beginning and ending of the ties. A good guide is to leave the twine loose enough to allow the hand to be slipped under the loops. Where bridle ties are used in stuffed and stitched work, the loops need to be looser to accommodate more filling.

The general principle in positioning 'bridle tie' loops in the hessian is that an amount of teased filling held in the hand will spread to approximately 15 cm (6 in.) in width, so working from an outer edge of the frame the first tie should be approximately 7.5 cm (3 in.) parallel with the edge. The tie will then be running down the centre of the filling being worked onto the seat. The next tie should be approximately 15 cm (6 in.) from the first and so on. It is advisable to work the outer 'bridle' ties into the hessian first, then infill the centre as appropriate.

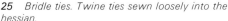

25 *Bridle ties. Twine ties sewn loosely into the hessian.*

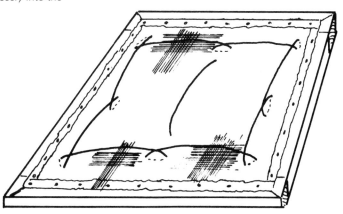

Adding the filling

After the filling has been thoroughly teased, it should be systematically tucked under the 'bridle' ties. Start in one corner and work round the four sides, leaving the centre to be completed last to obtain the correct amount of doming. It is essential that the filling be applied evenly with an eye to the final shape, which should not have an over-stuffed look. Filling for a 'drop in' seat should have a fairly flat appearance. Attention should be paid to the top edges of the seat frame to ensure that the filling extends to these, so that there are no bare spots which will allow the hard timber of the frame to be felt through the final covering.

Where new fillings are to be used, the teasing process may sometimes be needed to fully 'open' the strands. Original fillings may be re-usable if well teased, but frequently the quality and resilience of some of the older fillings other than horsehair leave a lot to be desired, and they should be discarded rather than be re-used.

Applying the undercovering

An undercovering of unbleached calico or similar material should be 'pulled' over the filling as the next step. This step is of great help in obtaining a successful finish. In order to keep the weave straight, centre marks should be put on the front and back edges of the undercovering. These should then be lined up with centre marks on the underside of the seat frame. 'Temporary' tacking, using 1.2 cm ($\frac{1}{2}$ in.) fine tacks in the order shown in figure 26, is necessary while the calico is being correctly tensioned.

Correct tensioning of the undercovering is important. If left too slack it tends to fold under the top covering causing unevenness, and soil lines will appear on the surface where the folds of the undercovering are standing proud. Too tight a tensioning of the calico will diminish the resilience of the filling causing too firm a seat to be produced. A suitable test to determine correct tension is to gently press the fingers of each hand on to the surface of the calico at each side of the seat, then move the hands towards the centre of the seat. If the tension is correct no loose folds of material will gather between the tips of the fingers as they meet. Should the calico be too slack the looseness will be gathered between the fingers. Once the undercovering is correctly tensioned, it can be tacked home with 1 cm ($\frac{3}{8}$ in.) fine tacks on the face edges of the seat frame.

26 Sequence of temporary tacking. Calico and covering should be tensioned in the direction of the arrows.

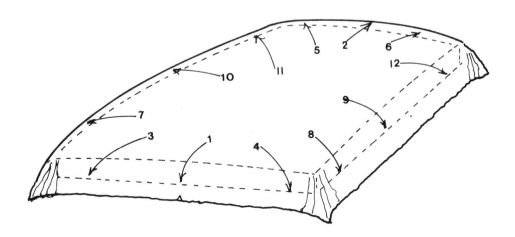

Inserting the wadding

If the filling used is horsehair or hair mixture, cotton wadding should be placed over the calico undercovering before applying the final covering fabric. Wadding should cover the surface only up to the top edges; the side face edges should be kept free so that only the calico and covering are between the seat frame and rebate. The purpose of the wadding is to prevent the strands of horsehair from working through the calico and covering at a later date. Wadding will also give an added softness or quilted effect to the covering.

Where a non-horsehair filling has been used, such as a cotton felt, some form of felted mixture, or even foam, the wadding can be omitted if desired. This is also true of the calico undercovering. The work will, however, be better for the inclusion of both these stages.

Placing and finishing the top covering

The final covering, of course, is all-important. A misaligned, wrongly placed and badly finished covering will mar the work. Care taken in this operation will be amply repaid.

First the covering must be centred so that the warp and weft threads are running parallel with the edges and straight down the centre of the seat. Where the fabric has a motif it should be temporarily tacked and checked before the final tacking takes place. Temporary tacking should be with 1.2 cm ($\frac{1}{2}$ in.) fine tacks, and the final tacking with 1 cm ($\frac{3}{8}$ in.) fine tacks.

Care should be taken with pleating the fabric at the corners. Surplus covering under the pleats should be cut away to reduce the thickness of the folded material (figure 27). If this step is omitted, there is a risk that the seat will not fit into the rebate at the corners. Remember, if the seat will not fit after covering, on no account use force to make it fit into the rebate. It is far easier to make a minor alteration to the seat than a major repair to the polished chair joint. Spacing of tacks for holding the covering should be approximately 3 cm ($1\frac{1}{4}$ in.).

27   Treatment of corners. Method of tacking, cutting and pleating covering. Pleats should be on the front and back corners.

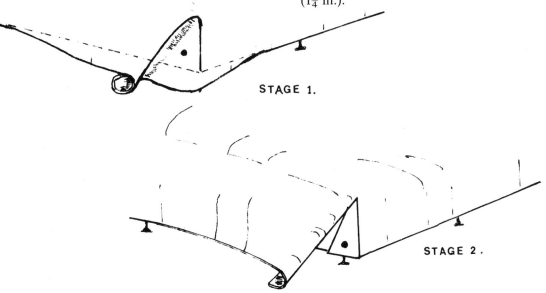

STAGE 1.

STAGE 2.

After the top covering has been tacked, all surplus material should be cut away to allow the 'bottoming' to be tacked on. This can be any type of light-weight fabric which will give a neat and tidy appearance to the underside of the seat; 1 cm ($\frac{3}{8}$ in.) tacks spaced approximately 4 cm ($1\frac{1}{2}$ in.) apart, can be used on a seat such as this. They should be positioned at the extreme edge of the folded material so that the fold will lie flat and not roll up. The folded edge of the bottoming should be approximately 8 to 10 mm ($\frac{1}{4}$ to $\frac{3}{8}$ in.) in from the outer edge.

STRIPPING UPHOLSTERY

Assessment of work

Before an attempt is made to strip down old upholstery, a thorough examination of the piece should be made to ascertain the extent of necessary re-upholstery. With some of the larger pieces it may be possible to retain parts of the filling and stitching in their original positions, provided the base suspension hessian and webbing has not deteriorated very much. There are certain parts of upholstered work which are not load-bearing and are not therefore reliant on the strength of the webbing and hessian as are the load-bearing parts. The parts which do not need removing are those where the supporting webbing and hessian have retained their original tautness, whereas the load-bearing webs will have stretched and be sagging to a degree. A careful appraisal of the work prior to and during the process of stripping can save a large amount of labour and money in replacement of materials without affecting the quality of the restoration work.

If on removal the covering is complete, it can be used as a template or pattern in cutting the new covering fabric. It can also be a great help in estimating the quantity of new fabric required. By laying the old covering out on a table or on the floor it is possible to establish how the material was originally cut from the full width of cloth. It may be found that two identical pieces, for example, the two inside or two outside arms, or the inside and outside back, may have been cut from the full width, and faced together making a pair; this frequently is the case.

An additional advantage of retaining the old covering is that it is a good guide to the overall dimensions of the original upholstery, particularly where the old fillings have been completely stripped away and discarded, and have to be rebuilt. The restored upholstery should, of course, follow as near as possible the original lines. Generally the old covering will have wear or soil lines where the leading edges have had the hardest wear, also the covering tends to fade or discolour in areas which have been exposed. These are lines which are very useful in establishing the depth of seats and backs, and depths of stitched edges.

Further, where deep buttoned work is being restored, the original covering will be invaluable in re-marking the 'ground work' (button positions) and establishing the amount of 'fullness' when marking the covering to give the correct diamond pleating between the buttons. So it is especially important in this instance to remove the former covering carefully, cutting the old twine ties holding the buttons in position without tearing or cutting the covering from the back or seat.

In addition to making an initial assessment of the upholstery needing refurbishing, it is necessary to check whether any repairs are needed to the timber frame. A well constructed frame of beech will generally stand up to normal wear and tear for a considerable number of years, so in many instances it will be found that the frame of the piece is sound. In order to test the rigidity of an easy chair frame the two arms should be firmly gripped and tested for any lateral movement in the joints of the frame. The back can be tested for any forward or backward movement by gripping one of the chair arms and holding the top of the back. Framework repairs to an easy chair or settee will often necessitate the removal of more of the original upholstery than would be the case if the frame were sound.

Sequence of work

It is advisable to approach the work of stripping in a systematic way. Done haphazardly the work is far more difficult, and the inexperienced person will have difficulty in following a logical sequence of operations. Generally, stripping should be carried out in reverse order to which the item was originally upholstered. With a careful approach to the work this should become apparent.

Stripping upholstery is a dusty operation better done in a workshop or garage. If it is attempted inside a house the floor should be liberally covered by dustsheets, not only to catch dust but to collect and contain the hundreds of tacks which need to be removed. The stripping of smaller items, such as loose seats and small chairs, can be done on a table or bench of suitable working height. For working on larger items a pair of trestles is much more convenient giving much easier access to the various parts of the work than a table. Certainly trestles are a good investment for the professional worker.

Any damage caused to the frame whilst stripping it of the old covering and filling will need to be repaired before re-upholstery, so, when using the ripping chisel, ensure that no pieces of timber break away from the frame, particularly at the corners. The old tacks should be taken out with the ripping chisel working in the direction of the grain of the timber. Place the blade of the chisel against the head of the tack, or under the material being held by the tack, with the chisel at a fairly low angle to pre-

vent the blade from being forced into the timber as it is hit with the mallet (plate 23). The tacks will normally be standing a little proud with the fabric, hessian or webbing under them, and two or three taps with the mallet on the end of the handle of the ripping chisel will remove most tacks. The mallet, as mentioned earlier, should always be used on the wooden handle of any chisel to avoid splitting the wood which would occur if a steel hammer were used.

A few of the smaller tacks may have been hammered deep into the grain of the timber making them difficult to remove. As they will not interfere with the finish these may be left provided the old fabric or whatever they held is completely removed, so that a flat surface is left on the face of the timber.

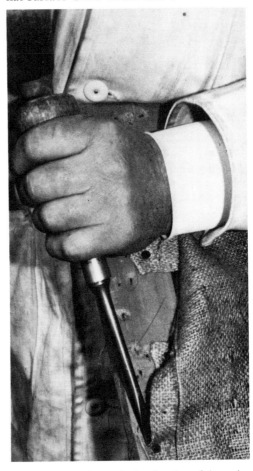

23 Ripping tacks out in the direction of the grain of the timber.

Tacks at the corner of a frame should be ripped out inwards towards the centre of the item. If they are removed and forced out near the edges of the timber, damage will invariably occur as pieces will break away or split (figure 28). On no account should tacks be chopped out for quickness with the claw side of the upholsterer's hammer. This practice will tear the grain and leave large splinters of wood which may be dangerous to the hands. Also, there is a very real chance of breaking a large piece of timber away. Patience at this stage of the work will have its just rewards.

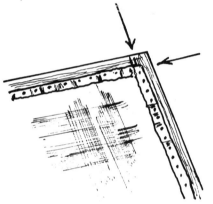

28   *Ripping inwards from corner.*

Most traditional work will have a 'bottoming', that is, an undercovering on the base of the chair or seat. It may be of any type of material: black linen, black dyed hessian, natural coloured hessian, or white calico. The purpose of this is to neaten the underside by hiding the raw edges of the upholstery covering. It also contains any dust or fragments of filling from the loose stuffing used in the chair, preventing them from falling on to floor or carpets. The bottoming needs to be removed as the first operation. Tacks used to hold this are usually of the lighter variety and not difficult to take out. The easiest method is to upturn the chair or settee so that the base is uppermost, the top of the back is resting on the floor, and a stool or trestle is supporting the seat (plate 24).

After removal of the bottoming, the tacked edges of the covering will be exposed. Whilst the item is still in an upside-down position, it is convenient to remove the tacks holding the covering. With the larger items the 'outside' back, 'outside' arms and front border can be released at this stage. Frequently the 'outside' back and 'outside' arms will also be slip-stitched (figure 9 on page 28), or sewn with strong thread along the corners from top to bottom of the piece. This needs snipping, which will then allow the method of tacking along the top edge to be seen – normally back-tacking (figure 5 on page 24).

It is usual with a well upholstered easy chair or settee to find a reinforcing layer of hessian tacked under the covering. The object of this is to prevent distortion of the stretched covering should any pressure be applied from the outside, for example, if in moving or handling the piece something is inadvertently pressed into the covering. It is a good practice, well worth repeating in the refurbishing of the piece. In stripping for re-upholstery this hessian will, of course, need to be removed.

After removal of the outside coverings, the order of stripping the insides will generally be: inside back and facing (where applicable), inside arms (and facings), border and seat. There are, of course, hundreds of styles of upholstered pieces. It is difficult to lay down hard and fast rules for all work of this nature, but a little careful investigation will often present you with the best logical method of stripping down a chair or settee.

When refurbishing work where the basic construction, and perhaps the top stuffing, do not need stripping, it is advisable to leave the inside coverings in position after removing the old tacks. Leave the odd temporary tack here and there to hold the covering; this will prevent the filling from becoming displaced. The covering can then be quickly removed at the appropriate time.

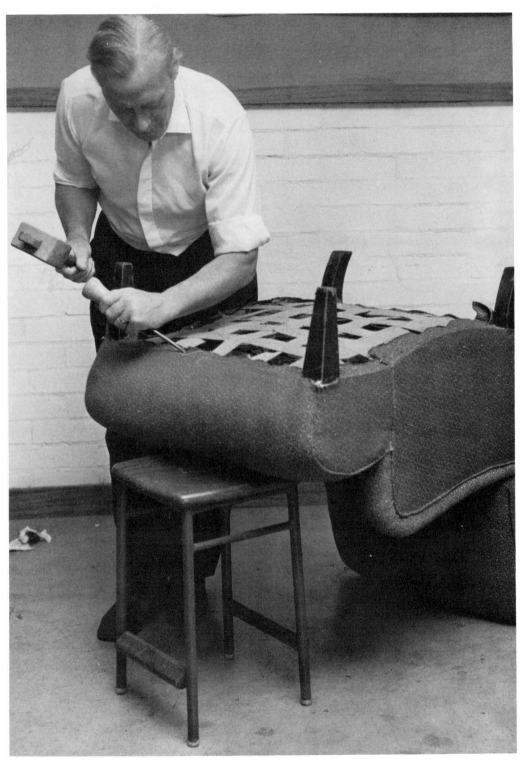

24 Stripping the covering off with chair upside down for ease of working.

Where a sprung seat obviously needs replacing, it is wise to renew *all* the seat springs. There may be some amongst the group of springs which, over the years of use, have become distorted or 'crippled'. These distorted springs should *not* be straightened and re-used. The coils of the springs will have become misaligned and the wire weakened. If re-used, they will in a very short space of time become distorted again, resulting in a further lengthy and costly repair.

The types of fillings which can be successfully re-used in re-upholstery work are fairly limited. A carding machine, which is essential for the 'opening' of matted fillings, such as horsehair or hair mixtures and fibres of various types, is seldom available to the amateur or small professional repairer. It is a case of 'teasing' or opening the filling by hand to enable it to recover its original resilience, a long, dusty and rather unpleasant task, or disposing of the original fillings and replacing. In 'teasing' the filling it is essential to open the strands or fibres thoroughly, and not leave any matted portions. It is possible, of course, to card hair as it was done in the early days of the upholsterer, before the advent of the machine. It was done with two wooden 'bat' shaped boards with nails protruding. These were faced together with the matted horse hair between, and, after a degree of rubbing together, the hair was combed. Older upholstered pieces invariably contain a good proportion of high grade horse mane and cattle tail hair, this being very long stranded with a good deal of curl, and very springy. Such a filling is always well worth reclaiming. Time spent on hand teasing is time well spent as hair of this quality nowadays is difficult to obtain and very expensive.

25 'Stuffover' upholstered easy chair.

FRAME REPAIRS

The basic frame

It is essential for the basic upholstery frame to be made of hard wood to hold successfully the tacks or staples (used in modern construction). If soft woods are used, tacks very quickly become loose and work out with the tension of the various covering fabrics. It is sometimes found that to reduce costs soft wood has been used for additional shaping pieces on part of a frame which is taking no strain, or on which no tacking is required. That is as far as soft wood should be used in upholstered items. Beech is the timber most favoured by the specialist maker of stuffover frames (upholstery frames completely covered except for a very small area of polished wood, for example, the feet (plate 25). Show wood frames (constructed with polished arms or an amount of polished finish) may have some other timber used in the show wood area, for example, walnut or oak (plate 26).

26 A 'show-wood' upholstered easy chair.

Checking and repairing joints

It is vitally important that all joints on the frame are sound. Unlike a cabinet or sideboard which usually stands in one position throughout its life, the upholstery frame undergoes many strains and stresses with the tensions of the materials tacked upon it, and from the movements of the sitting person. When pieces are re-sited they are often picked up and dropped on a corner of the frame. Consequently a poorly constructed frame could have a comparatively short life.

As mentioned earlier on page 42, the rigidity of the frame can be tested before the upholstery is stripped as an indication of the amount of work involved. But only when the coverings are removed is it possible to observe the actual condition of the frame. The frame may be found to have more movement in the joints owing to the removal of materials binding it together. Some joints may even be well open. Wherever possible, these should be either completely eased open or knocked apart, the old glue removed, damaged dowels replaced, the joint re-glued, drawn together, and sash cramped for 24 hours.

The dowelled joint normally used for upholstery frame making is stronger than other types of joints and easier to produce by machine drilling and cramping. One, two or three 1 cm ($\frac{3}{8}$ in.) beech dowels may be used depending upon the section or thickness of the rails in the particular joint (figure 29). Soft wood certainly will not give the housing strength to encase the dowel to make a rigid and durable joint.

The mortice and tenon joint may be encountered in restoration work. Such a joint may have become slack owing to a broken tenon or mortice which will need repairing. Or the joint may be dry, the glued surfaces having come apart: these will need regluing and cramping after removing the old glue from the joint. Where this treatment is not possible, which it frequently is not, an alternative treatment is reinforce-

ment of slack joints and frame corners with flat steel straight or right-angled plates which must be securely screwed in position (plates 27 and 28).

A further alternative is the use of plywood gussets which may either be triangular, oblong or L-shaped to accommodate the joint in need of repair. These gussets are glued then screwed into position (plates 29 and 30).

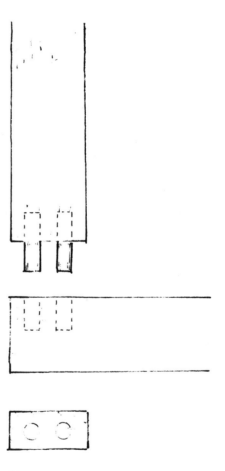

29 The dowelled joint. Exploded view of a two pin joint as used in loose seat construction.

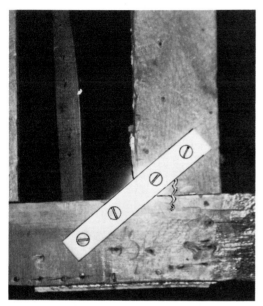

27 Flat steel reinforcing plate with corrugated fastener in position to strengthen joint.

28 Use of right-angled steel plate strengthening wing.

29 Plywood gusset strengthening wing upright member.

30 Plywood gussets and flat steel plates used in conjunction.

Dealing with woodworm

Also important in the restoration of the frame is to watch for signs of woodworm which may be still active. In older styles these often occur on the underside of the frame, usually on the inner faces of the sides and ends where the upholstery has been 'top stuffed' leaving the timber bare. Timber pests rarely attack wood which has a polished finish, but are often found in crevices or parts which have been missed by the polisher: in ridges of carving is another example. The holes in which the pests are active will appear fairly light-coloured compared with other exit holes, and an amount of wood dust will be apparent, either on the floor below the affected part or will drop out of the holes when the timber is tapped.

The only real cure for affected timber is to cut away completely the affected part and destroy it. As this is rarely possible, the next best treatment is to totally strip the area of any upholstery, and inject into the worm holes a proprietary brand of woodworm killer: an injector is usually supplied. It is most important to follow the manufacturer's instructions, particularly those concerning the use of the solution in an enclosed area. In many cases it may be found that only one member of the frame has been affected. After the affected part has been well-soaked, it should be allowed to dry out before re-upholstery is attempted.

31 3 × 3 webbs applied tacked with 1.2 cm ($\frac{1}{2}$″) improved tacks.

32 12 oz hessian tacked over webbing — edges of hessian to be folded over.

THE 'TOP STUFFED' SEAT

Method of work

Plates 31 to 43 show a number of stages in the upholstery of a 'top stuffed' show wood dressing stool. The term 'top stuffed' means that the interior upholstery is applied to the top of the seat only. No form of springing, which would require webbing to be attached to the base of the seat rails, is included within the frame. Work on this stool is identical to the stages illustrated in figures 30 to 37 showing the method of forming each of the stitches on a small chair seat.

Before attempting upholstery, ensure that there is a bevel on the outer top edge of the seat members. If the frame is being re-upholstered, the bevel may already be made, but may need cleaning up. If a new frame is being used there may be no bevel: this can quickly and easily be made with a coarse wood rasp.

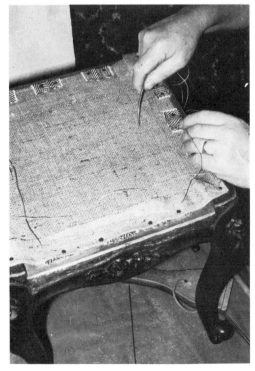

33 Sewing 'bridle' ties into position using a spring needle.

34 Putting the 'first' stuffing under the bridle ties.

Positioning the webbing

Plate 31 shows the positioning of the webbing, three by three strands being used as the seat is square with sides of equal length. The method and sequence of applying the webbing should be followed as in figure 24 on page 38, but adding one more strand. Improved tacks of 1.2 cm ($\frac{1}{2}$ in.) length should be used in tacking the webbing.

Care should be taken when using the 'bat' webbing strainer to avoid bruising the polished show wood. The rebated edge of the web strainer should, where possible, be rested upon the unpolished rebate of the frame. In some instances it may be found that the rebate is too narrow to support the strainer and in order to tension the webbing, the strainer may have to be used against the polished surface. In this situation, a soft pad of wadding should be used as an insulation between the base of the webbing strainer and the polished surface. It is advisable not to use a pad of hessian or any sort of woven cloth as the pressure of the strainer when tension is being applied will leave an imprint of the weave of the cloth upon the polished surface.

Applying the hessian

A good quality hessian should be stretched over the webbing, 1.2 cm ($\frac{1}{2}$ in.) fine tacks being used for this operation. The first edge of the hessian may be tacked approximately at 1.2 cm ($\frac{1}{2}$ in.) fold, the tacks being spaced about 3.5 to 4 cm ($1\frac{1}{4}$ to $1\frac{1}{2}$ in.) apart. The remaining three sides should be tacked singly, after the hessian has been tensioned as tight as possible by hand. The surplus hessian is then cut away leaving approximately 1.5 cm ($\frac{5}{8}$ in.) for the fold which is then tacked down with slightly wider spacing than were the tacks under the fold (plate 32).

In tacking the hessian in position a golden rule is to keep the threads of the weave straight, running parallel with the sides and front of the frame. Also, when beginning to tack start in the centre, then work progressively towards the sides. In this way all looseness is worked out to the corners. An exception to this rule is working a seat where the side members are tapered towards the back. In this instance, it is better to start tacking the hessian on the sides at the front working towards the back.

Having tacked the hessian in place, 'bridle' ties should be inserted using a 'spring' needle (plate 33, and figure 25 on page 39), two loops being sufficient along each side, with two down the centre (one way only). These 'bridle' ties should be left slack enough to allow a handful of filling to be tucked under. If the ties are put in too tightly they may be pulled away whilst infilling with stuffing, breaking the jute yarn from which the hessian is woven.

The first stuffing

This filling which may be hair or fibre should now be teased and tucked under the 'bridle' ties evenly and smoothly (plate 34), starting at one corner, working along one side to the opposite corner, then the remaining three sides, after which the centre area is filled in. The filling around the outer edges should be fairly dense but not solidly packed. This upholstery technique is probably one of the most difficult to master, and can only be learned by experience. The skilled craftsman can generally gauge the correct amount of filling without having to add more to the edges at a later stage. The appearance of the first stuffing should be reasonably flat on the top surface with slight doming in the centre, the filling should have a lively feel after having been teased.

Upholsterer's scrim should now be *temporarily* tacked with 1.2 cm ($\frac{1}{2}$ in.) improved tacks allowing three to four tacks along each side. On no account tack the scrim down in the first instance. Ensure that the weave of the scrim is lying parallel with the sides of the frame. Failure to do this will result in difficulty in stitching the edges straight. With the scrim temporarily tacked, ties to hold the stuffing firmly in position should be inserted into it. This stage is shown in plate 35, and in figure 30 on a small chair seat with the same type of upholstery.

Stout twine should be employed for the stuffing ties. Use a 20 to 25 cm (8 to 10 in.) bayonet needle, and make sure the twine penetrates the scrim from the top, through the filling, and out through the hessian on the base; then push the twine back through the hessian a short distance away (approximately 0.5 cm ($\frac{1}{4}$ in.)), and out through the surface of the scrim.

Through the scrim and base hessian a slip-knot (figure 11 on page 31) should be made at the first position to hold the twine fast, then, having previously marked positions for the ties by stabbing the scrim with the point of the needle, continue inserting the desired number of ties over the whole area. The outer lines of ties should be approximately 9 to 10 cm ($3\frac{1}{2}$ to 4 in.) in from the outer edges of the filling. Twine returning out of the scrim should be spaced away from the entry point in the direction of progress around the seat so that it is a running line, without any knotting or overlapping. Starting at the first knotted tie, ease the twine tight between each in turn, moving round by pressing the fingers along the lines of twines and depressing the surface of the scrim until the final tie is reached. This should have a temporary knot only, to allow for any adjustment needed at a later stage.

Prior to permanently tacking down the scrim, any adjustment needed to the filling should be done as the temporary tacks are removed. Edges of the scrim must be folded *under* with the tacks which hold the extreme folded edge sitting on the bevelled edge. The latter should be the same width as the heads of the tacks (figure 30 and plate 36). As the scrim is being tacked down, odd strands of filling or scrim should be tucked in with the aid of the flat end of the regulator, leaving a clean and tidy appearance. This is the hallmark of a master craftsman.

Permanent tacking of the scrim should be carried out with 0.9 cm ($\frac{3}{8}$ in.) improved tacks, or for a very fine weave scrim, 0.9 cm ($\frac{3}{8}$ in.) fine tacks may be used in their place. Spacing of tacks should be approximately 0.9 to 1 cm ($\frac{3}{8}$ in.) apart.

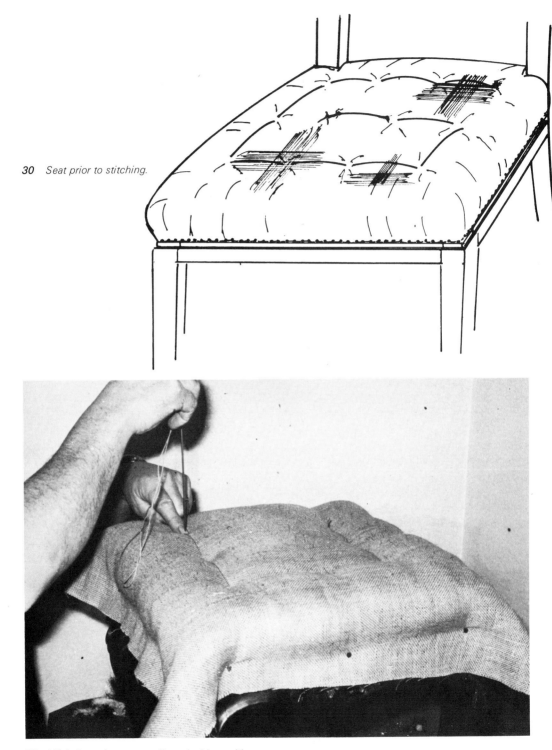

30 *Seat prior to stitching.*

35 With the scrim temporarily tacked in position, twine stuffing ties are run through with a 25.5 cm (10″) needle.

Types of stitching

Once the scrim has been completely tacked along each edge and corner, stitching should be considered. The number of rows of stitching required for any item depends upon the height of the edge. The illustrations in figures 31 to 37 and plates 37 and 38, show three rows of stitching, blind stitch, roll stitch and fine top stitch, these being a suitable number for that particular item with filling height of approximately 5 cm (2 in.). A shallower edge would need two rows only, blind and top stitch. To give stability to a higher edge four rows of stitching would be advisable with two blind, one roll and one top stitch. Generally it is not good practice to attempt to stuff and stitch too deep an edge, the filling will tend to reduce in height during the course of its life however well it has been upholstered. Where additional height is required, a length of timber should be screwed on the top edge of the frame so that its depth is increased, thus allowing for a shallower amount of filling.

Inserting the filling, tacking the scrim and stitching are probably the most difficult of all upholstery operations. These are part of the upholsterer's art, and the craftsman gains much satisfaction in producing an edge parallel to the weave of the scrim, and sufficiently firm (but not solid) to withstand constant use. Learners' first attempts in these operations will probably be disappointing to them. Where it is apparent that this stage has gone wrong, it is well worthwhile to re-attempt it as the success of the job depends a good deal on how this is done.

36 Scrim partly tacked down on bevelled edge.

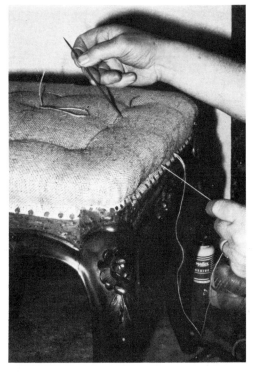

37 The first row of stitching being put in, this is the 'blind' stitch.

Owing to the complexity of the stitching, a number of diagrams and photographs have been included in this chapter to illustrate the various stages and type of stitch. Figures 31 to 34 and plate 37 on page 55 show blind stitching in detail. The purpose of the blind-stitch is to form a loop of twine within the filling. A bayonet needle 20 to 25 cm (8 to 10 in.) in length, is most suitable for this. Use a good quality stitching twine and insert the point of the needle into the scrim a little above its tacked line. Partly withdraw the needle approximately three-quarters of its length from the upper surface of the seat, just in front of the line of stuffing ties, as shown in figure 32. Now pass the needle back (figure 33) but whilst doing this, guide the leading point towards the left to carry the twine round in as wide a loop as possible within the filling, then allow the point of the needle to re-emerge approximately 1 cm ($\frac{3}{8}$ in.) to the left of

where it entered the scrim above the tacking line. Twist the twine to the left of the needle twice around it to form a double knot which should then not slip back when the loop is tightened (figure 34). Withdraw the needle completely. As the twine is gently eased tight the filling will be drawn forward to consolidate the edge, and the loop will keep the filling permanently in position. Blind-stitches should be approximately 3 to 4 cm ($1\frac{1}{4}$ to $1\frac{1}{2}$ in.) apart, and unnoticeable on the upper surface of the seat.

On completion of the blind-stitch, a roll-stitch should be made (figures 35 and 36), but before this is attempted the edge filling should be made as even as possible by the use of the regulator. It is very important for the edge to be evenly filled.

Again, use the bayonet needle for the roll-stitch. This time, take the needle and twine right through the scrim making stitches approximately 1 cm ($\frac{3}{8}$ in.) in length.

31   Blind stitch – Method of forming stitch. Stage 1.

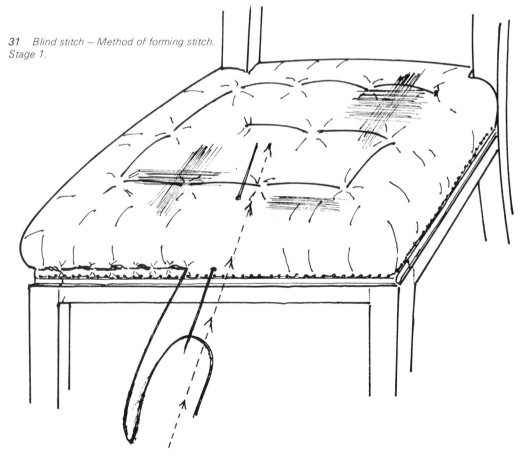

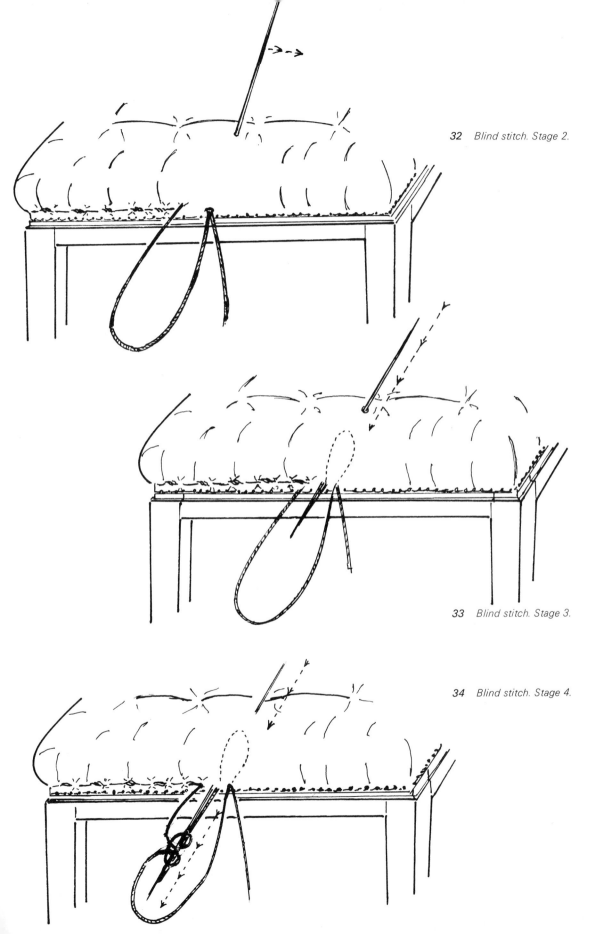

32 *Blind stitch. Stage 2.*

33 *Blind stitch. Stage 3.*

34 *Blind stitch. Stage 4.*

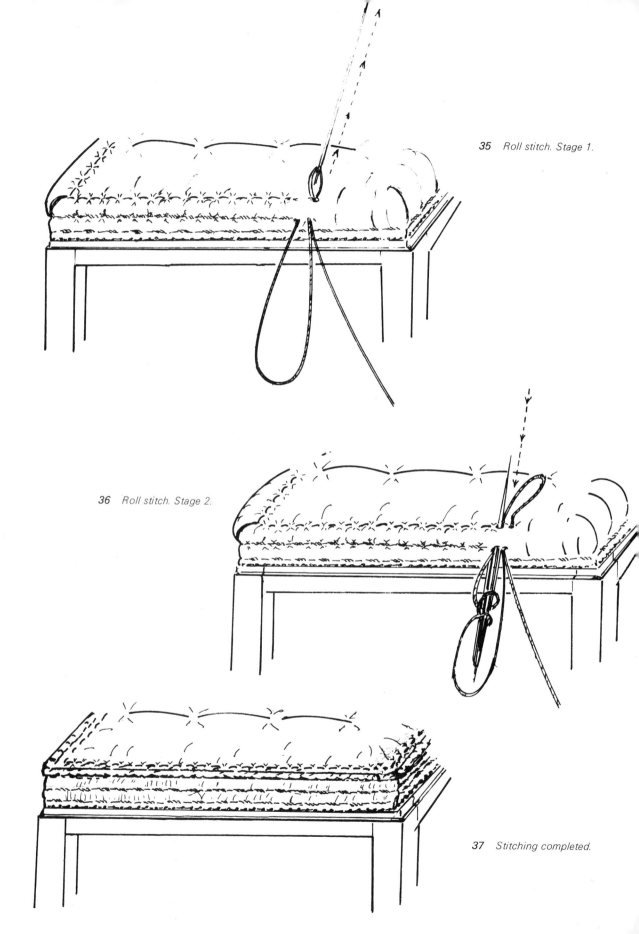

35 *Roll stitch. Stage 1.*

36 *Roll stitch. Stage 2.*

37 *Stitching completed.*

The ideal is to have each stitch adjacent without any spaces between. Where three stitches are being made they should be evenly spaced up the height of the edge, say, 1.2 cm ($\frac{1}{2}$ in.) apart. Decide at the beginning of the stitching operation what the finished height is to be, so that the stitching can be evenly spaced.

The last row of stitching should be fairly fine to give a sharp box-like edge to the seat (figure 37 and plate 38). This should be approximately half the size of the roll-stitch but much flatter. Again, the needle and twine are completely withdrawn through the top surface of the seat scrim. The aim throughout in stitching the seat is to make an edge which will appear perpendicular with the front rail when the final covering is on.

Final padding, covering, and finishing
When the stitching is completed, further bridle ties should be sewn into the surface of the scrim using a spring needle as for the base hessian. Plate 39 shows the second stuffing of hair mixture being tucked under the ties. It should be noted that the first stuffing is fairly flat; the second stuffing should also be kept reasonably flat and even to avoid that over-stuffed look which mars the final appearance so much.

The seat should now be pulled over in calico, lining material, or some other reasonably low priced fabric. Plate 40 shows the calico undercovering temporarily tacked in position, while plate 41 shows the calico completely tacked home. It is unnecessary to fold the material, it may be tacked singly on the raw edge with 1 cm ($\frac{3}{8}$ in.) fine tacks. The surplus material should be trimmed off close to the tacks.

38 Completing the final row of fine top stitching.

39 Second stuffing of hair being tucked under 'bridle' ties.

Whilst an undercovering is advisable, it can, if desired, be omitted where cutting costs and work time is important. The undercovering is beneficial where a fine or fragile top covering is to be used. The latter does not need to be tugged or strained into position because the final surface shape has already been made by the undercovering. Any upholstered work is better for this additional refinement; certainly any work covered in leather should be so treated.

To prevent the hair from eventually working through the top covering, lay cotton wadding over the surface of the calico, or if no undercovering is used, over the hair. At least two, preferably three, layers of skin wadding are needed, or, if skinless wadding is being used, a suitable thickness equal to three layers of skin wadding after splitting the 'lap'. Use the cellulose skin side of the wadding as the underside with the softer side uppermost. Trim away the wadding approximately half way down the sides of the seat, keeping it well clear of the tacking line.

The top covering should be cut to allow sufficient surplus on each side to work with. Where the covering fabric has a central motif, ensure that the fabric is cut to allow the motif to sit centrally on the seat. Mark the sides of the frame to facilitate centring the covering.

Plate 42 shows the temporary tacking of the covering, while plate 43 shows the covering tacked home with the gimp being applied. A cabriole hammer, which has a smaller face than an upholsterer's hammer, is being used to minimize the danger of hitting the polish whilst hammering the tack close to the finished edge. Fine tacks of 1 cm ($\frac{3}{8}$ in.) length are used to tack home the covering. Treatment for the corners which,

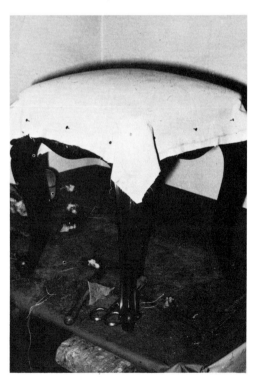

40 Calico 'temporary' tacked into position.

41 Calico tacked 'home' — 1 cm ($\frac{3}{8}$") fine tacks should be used.

in this case, have a fairly large radius should be a number of small pleats spread out evenly round the perimeter of the corner.

Use an adhesive to fix the gimp or braid. Thinly spread the adhesive (*not* the contact type) along the back surface of the trimming with a spatula or small brush, taking care not to over-apply. It must not run over the edges, or work through the weave. Whilst the adhesive is drying, small tacks or gimp pins can be used temporarily to hold the braid in place. These may be removed later.

The stool shown in plates 31 to 43 did not require a 'bottoming' piece, as the covering was finished on the sides of the frame. In cases where the covering is fixed to the underside of the frame a bottoming piece would be required to cover the raw edges of the fabric.

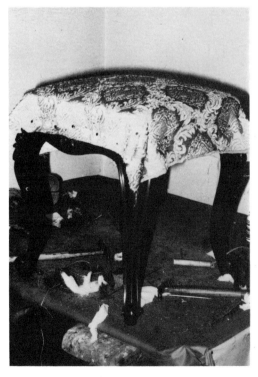

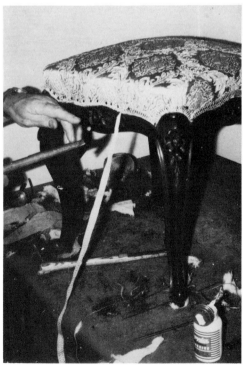

42   Covering positioned by temporary tacking.

43   Use of the cabriole hammer whilst applying the gimp.

SECTION THREE

Springing and Cushion Making

TRADITIONAL SPRINGING

A great deal can be written on the technicalities of upholstery springing, but for the purpose of this book I propose to limit the information to the bare essentials the restorer needs to know.

'Double cone' springing

The traditional 'double cone' spring (figure 38) will probably be the type that most readers will be dealing with, particularly where the upholstery is Victorian or pre-1940. The double cone spring, sometimes referred to as the 'waisted' or 'hour glass' spring, is used in hand-sprung work. It is sewn on to the base webbing (plate 44) with twine holding one of the large end coils firmly, the other large end coil being sewn to the covering hessian in a similar way after the hessian has been tacked in position over the surface of the springs (plate 45).

Upholstery springs are normally given anti-corrosion treatment by black lacquering, galvanizing or thinly coating with copper. Whilst the copper coating is to some extent rust resistant, if subjected to moisture or condensation, some rust will form roughening the surface of the wire. By causing wear on the hessian immediately touching the coil, this often results in hessian failure. As stressed earlier, old, crippled springs should not be straightened and re-used as the weakened wire will quickly become mis-shapen again and cause trouble.

The gauge of wire from which springs are made is all important. The gauge indicates the spring's softness or hardness. The lower numbered gauges make firmer springs than do the higher numbered gauges. As a

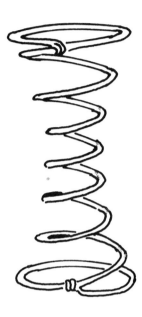

38   *Traditional double cone spring.*

general guide, the gauges suitable for seat use are $8\frac{1}{2}$, 9, $9\frac{1}{2}$ and 10 S.W.G. (standard wire gauge). A seat spring should be strong enough not to 'bottom' when sat on, that is, it should not completely close so that the sitter comes to rest upon the base webbing. The wider spaced upper and lower coils, being the softest part of the spring, should partially close first, then the closer centre coils should come into operation but remain sufficiently open to prevent the spring's complete collapse. Using too light a gauge spring in the seat suspension would allow all the coils to close at once. Gauges of $10\frac{1}{2}$ to 15 used for light, soft springs, are more suitable for the upholstery of backs and arms which need a lighter upholstered surface. Heights of springs obtainable range from 10 cm to 35 cm (4 to 14 in.).

Where restoration work is being undertaken, the original springs will give some guide to the height and gauge of the replacements needed. However, it may be impossible to obtain exactly similar replacements: in some of the older upholstered work the original springs are hand-made, incorporating heavier gauges of wire and more coils to each spring than is found in modern machine-made springing. The earlier hand-made springs can be identified by the fine wire binding on the ends of the wire of the larger coils to prevent them from penetrating the hessian, whereas the present day coil springs have the ends of the wire knotted mechanically. Where hand-made springs need replacing, use the nearest machine-made equivalent.

To give many years of trouble-free service double cone springs must be correctly placed and installed. A badly sprung seat will soon need re-upholstering. Figure 39, which represents a small easy chair seat, shows the ideal positions for the strands of webbing to support nine springs. Twelve springs may be used in larger easy chair seats. Where two or three seater settees are being worked, this number is usually doubled or trebled. It will be noticed that the lengths of webbing have been tacked in pairs close together so that the base coil of each spring is sitting on four webs. Some upholsterers, however, favour spacing all the strands out equally in both directions. This can be just as satisfactory provided the base of each spring has ample webbing to rest upon.

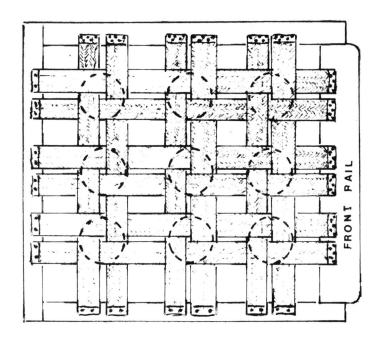

39 Webbing and springing. Siting of webbing and springs on easy chair seat. Webb is put on underside of frame.

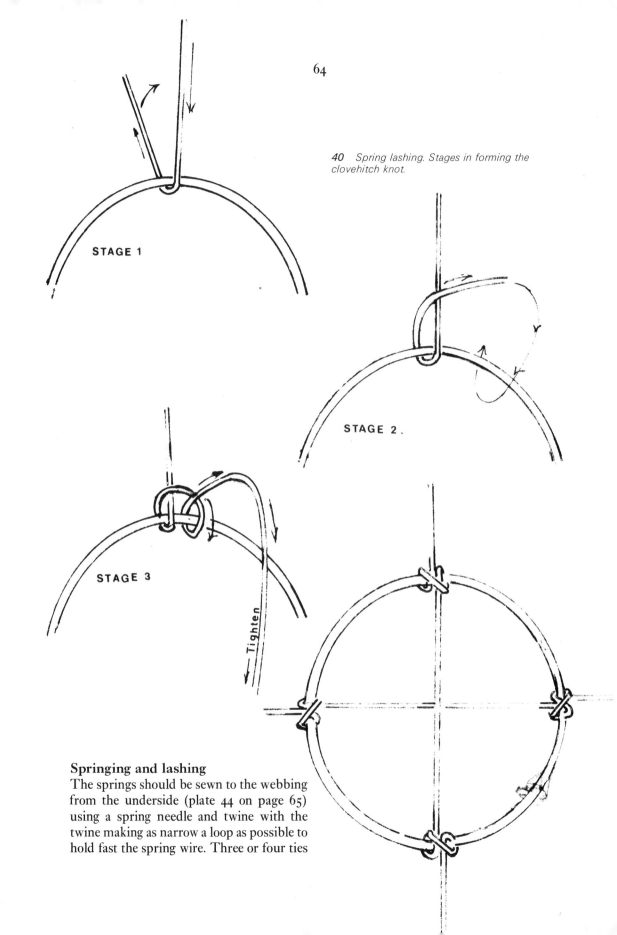

STAGE 1

40 Spring lashing. Stages in forming the clovehitch knot.

STAGE 2.

STAGE 3

Tighten

Springing and lashing

The springs should be sewn to the webbing from the underside (plate 44 on page 65) using a spring needle and twine with the twine making as narrow a loop as possible to hold fast the spring wire. Three or four ties may be used. Each individual tie should be knotted on the underside of the webbing by making one turn of twine around the spring needle as it is withdrawn. This small operation should not be missed out, as, without it, if the twine breaks at some time, the springs may shift about on the webbing. The ties should be made with a continuous length of twine, progressing from spring to spring across each row until completed. It is not advisable to work with an over long length of twine as it tends to become entangled and knotted. In practice it will be found that a convenient length to work with will sew approximately half the number of springs in an easy chair seat.

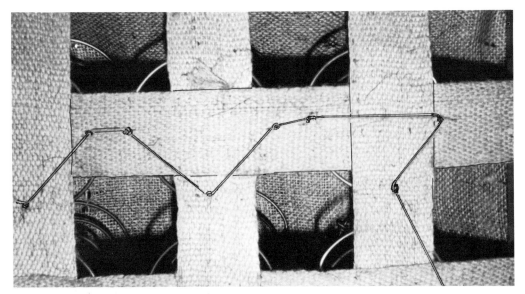

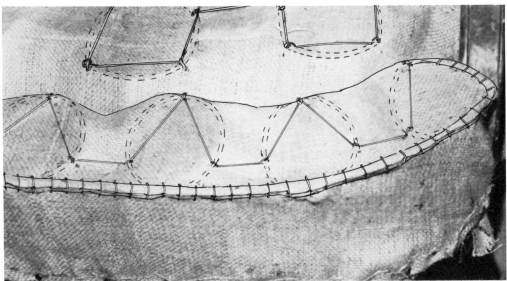

44 Showing base coils of springs sewn to the underside of the webbed seat.

45 Showing top coil of springs sewn through the hessian. Cane on spring edge is also closely sewn to the hessian.

Figures 40 to 46 show various stages in springing and lashing. The object of the lashing of a sprung seat or back is to make sure that there is only movement vertically with no lateral play whatsoever. A good quality laidcord should be used for this operation to ensure durability. The various stages in forming the clovehitch knot are shown in figure 40. Other knots are frequently used by upholsterers but the clovehitch is the most reliable, and easy to form after a little practice.

The section through the sprung seat (figure 41) shows the arrangement of springs for a 'sprung edge' seat, with shorter springs sitting on the front rail. It will be noted that the row of springs immediately behind the edge springs and also the back row of springs are lashed slightly out of straight, the front row slightly forward and the back row slightly leaning towards the back. This also applies to the two outside side rows from front to back. This counteracts the centre-pull tension to which the springs are subjected when sat upon.

41 Sprung edge easy chair seat. Lashing of springs using laidcord.

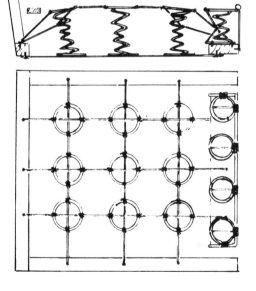

Where fairly tall springs are being used (say 9 in. or taller) in very deeply sprung work, it is advisable to double lash with additional lines of laidcord, lashing through the centres of the springs in both directions (figure 42). Single lashing across the crowns only of the higher springs tends to leave the long centre section coils free to bend and cripple whilst they are being compressed. The additional centre lashing should be laced through on to the springs after the top lashing has been completed and when the springs have been set to the desired height. When centre lashing, it is not necessary to return the ends of the cord to the crown coil of the spring: they may be cut off where tacked to the frame.

42 Double lashing of springs.

Fixing the edge springs

Figures 43 to 45 and plate 46 show details of the fixing of the edge springs and cane. A great deal of tension is applied to a sprung edge throughout its life: if not well constructed and firmly fixed it will have a short life. A better quality edge would have upholsterer's flexible cane lashed to the springs, but a heavy gauge spring wire is frequently used as a cheaper substitute which is not so satisfactory. The edge springs may be fixed in position with either 1.5 cm ($\frac{5}{8}$ in.) galvanized wire staples, or with a length of webbing stretching from arm to arm laid over the base coils of the springs and fixed with 1.5 cm ($\frac{5}{8}$ in.) improved tacks (figure 43).

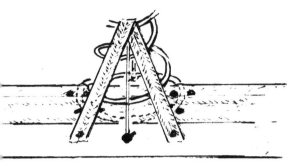

43 *Fixing of edge springs. Use of webbing to stabilize the spring. Spring fixed to rail using tacks.*

In constructing the spring edge, laidcord in an inverted V shape may be used to hold the springs forward (figure 45), or a half width of webbing may be used for the same purpose (figure 44). Either of these methods is acceptable.

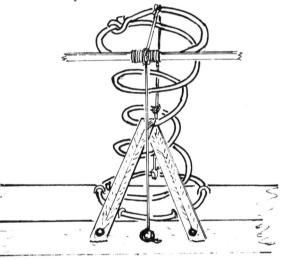

44 *Fixing of edge springs. Tying of spring and lashing the cane. Spring fixed to rail with staples.*

It will be noted that the cane which is used to create a continuous flexible straight line along the front of the edge springs has a right-angled bend at each end to carry it around the end springs of the edge (figures 41 and 45). To bend successfully, the cane must be fresh and pliable: a stiff, dry cane frequently splits or breaks during this process. Plate 47 shows the cane being bent.

A piece of iron gas piping and gentle heat from the flame of a candle are used as aids to getting as sharp an angle as possible. Great care must be taken during this operation. As the majority of commodities used in upholstery are highly flammable, it is advisable to do the cane bending well away from the area of normal work to avoid any danger of fire.

The secret of success in cane bending is to moisten the cane before attempting to bend it, and, whilst holding the cane above a gentle flame (from a candle or fine gas jet) to apply pressure gradually until a right angle has been formed. Prior to bending, a small V shape should be taken out of the cane with a rasp, the V being at the inside of the right angle. Before attempting to bend the length of cane you are to use for the edge, try a practice bend. This operation is particularly difficult, and it is frustrating if the piece you have cut to size breaks, and has to be discarded.

Some readers may wish to take the easy course and use heavy gauge wire instead of cane. Wire is easier to bend to a right angle but does not make such a satisfactory edge. Whichever method is used, either the cane or wire must be very firmly lashed to the front of the top coil of the edge spring (figure 45) with a number of turns of twine firmly knotted off.

45 *The easy chair spring edge. Completed spring edge.*

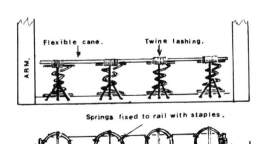

Flexible cane. Twine lashing.

ARM.

Springs fixed to rail with staples.

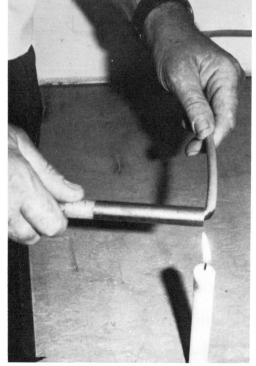

46 Showing seat springs lashed and edge springs in position.

47 Bending spring edge cane.

After the operation of lashing the springs in the 'well' of the seat and securing those on the edge, a covering of good quality hessian must be laid over them. As a spring edge operates independently of the springs in the well of the seat, the hessian should not be taken straight across from the back to the front: a 'gutter' should be formed, as shown in figure 46, so that the hessian sinks down approximately 5 to 6 cm (2 to $2\frac{1}{2}$ in.) deep between the two rows of springs. It is held in place with laidcord laced through and tacked to the base front rail. The edges of the hessian are then secured with 1.5 cm ($\frac{5}{8}$ in.) tacks. The hessian is tacked singly first, the surplus trimmed away, and the hessian folded and tacked again.

Spring units may also be used in back upholstery or three or four springs may be attached to a single metal lath nailed to the back members of the frame.

One or more of the springs may have become crippled or damaged in some way, or perhaps the whole unit may be unserviceable. The average reader will not be in a position to obtain replacement units as they are normally supplied only to upholstery manufacturers, and to replace single damaged springs in the unit is often not practical. It is generally more prudent to discard the complete unit, and replace it with normal webbing and double cone springs, ensuring that the replacement springs are of a suitable height to bring the finished upholstery to the original line.

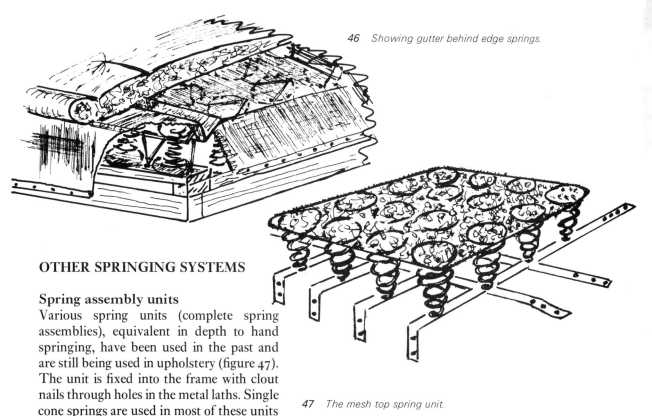

46 *Showing gutter behind edge springs.*

OTHER SPRINGING SYSTEMS

Spring assembly units

Various spring units (complete spring assemblies), equivalent in depth to hand springing, have been used in the past and are still being used in upholstery (figure 47). The unit is fixed into the frame with clout nails through holes in the metal laths. Single cone springs are used in most of these units (figure 48), although the better quality ones are constructed with double cone springs.

47 *The mesh top spring unit.*

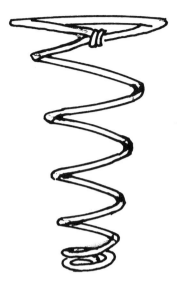

Tension or cable springs

An alternative system for the springing of seats and backs of chairs and settees is by tension or cable springs (figure 49). These are long thin springs, approximately 1.2 cm ($\frac{1}{2}$ in.) in diameter, tensioned across the frame and hooked by each end on to steel plates, one plate being screwed on each side member of the seat. Usually there are nine springs running across the seat or back. While upright coil springs are compression operated, tension springs expand when load is applied. Standing or placing too heavy a load on these springs causes them to become overstretched and distorted (plate 48).

48   *The single cone spring.*

49   *Tension springing.*

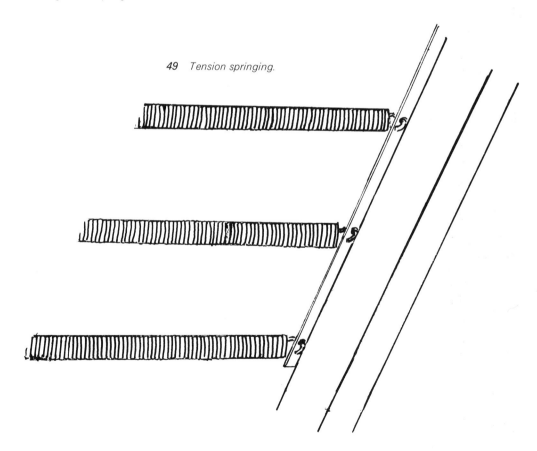

As they are usually visible when fixed in position on upholstery, tension springs are often manufactured with woven yarn or plastic sleeve covers. The plastic sleeving often splits through ageing or through the over-stretching of the spring, and the bare wire coils become visible. Apart from looking unsightly, these faults cause extra wear on the cushion covering resting upon the springs.

Where this type of springing has become unserviceable, it is a relatively simple job to replace all the springs with laminated rubber webbing. Since both are flat suspension systems needing no insulation over, they are readily interchangeable. The tension springs are easily removed from the holding plates, and these, in turn, can be unscrewed from the seat frame members without difficulty (plate 49).

48 Overstretched and damaged tension springs.

49 Removal of tension springs from their fixing
plates.

For seats 5 cm (2 in.) wide standard laminated rubber webbing is most suitable, and 3.8 cm (1½ in.), for backs. As the load-bearing surface area of the rubber webbing is much greater than that of the tension springs, the same number of strands as springs is not necessary. Approximately 4 cm (1½ in.) between the strands is suitable spacing. The webbing can be applied in the same direction as the springs were fixed (plate 50). When tacking it in position use 1.2 cm (½ in.) fine tacks. For the 5 cm (2 in.) webbing use four tacks each end. The tacks must be hammered home with the heads flat (figure 50) so that they do not cut into the rubber and weaken its holding power. The reinforcing rayon threads within the laminations of the webbing make it unnecessary to fold the ends back after tacking, as is usual with soft upholstery webbing. The tension of the webbing can be varied according to whether a firm or soft seat is desired. Average tension would be 7½ to 10 per cent stretch. The method of applying the tension is shown in plates 51 and 52.

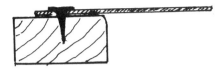

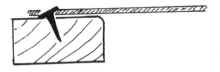

50 *Heads of tacks must be hammered flat. Lower illustration shows faulty tacking.*

50 Rubber webbing replacing damaged tension springs. Sharp inner edge of seat frame member must be rounded off.

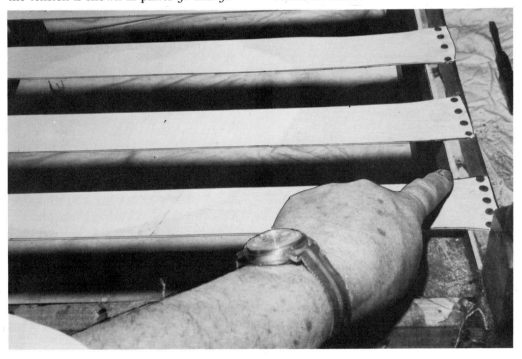

51 Marking rubber webbing and frame to equalize tension of each strand of webbing.

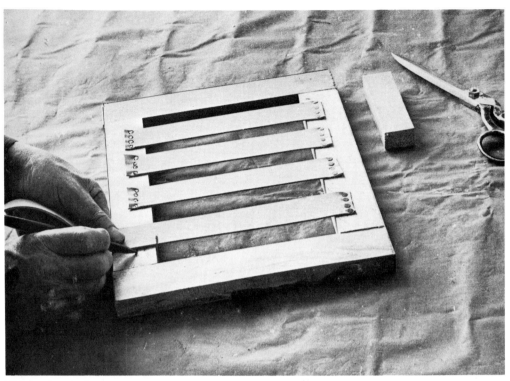

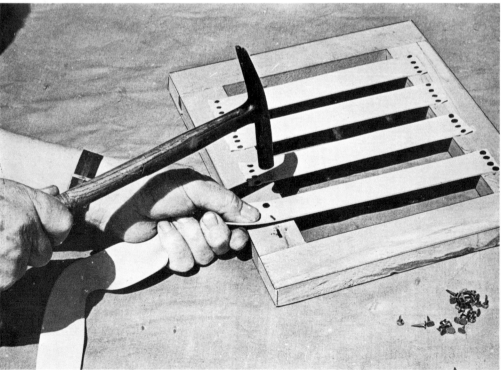

52 Tensioning the rubber webbing. Tensioning marks should now coincide.

Serpentine springing

Serpentine or sinuous springing (figures 51 and 52 and plate 53) is used extensively in contemporary upholstery production, and gives a fairly flat suspension, although not quite so flat as tension springing or rubber webbing. It has an inbuilt camber of approximately 3 to 6.5 cm ($1\frac{1}{4}$ to $2\frac{1}{2}$ in.) which gives a degree of doming to the seat or back, when the springing is fixed in position. Gauges obtainable are from 8 to 11 S.W.G., the heavier gauges being used for seats. Serpentine springing is supplied in cut lengths or by the roll for mass production use. There are a number of trade names by which it is known.

This type of springing most frequently breaks at or near the steel plate which clamps the end loop to the frame (figure 51).

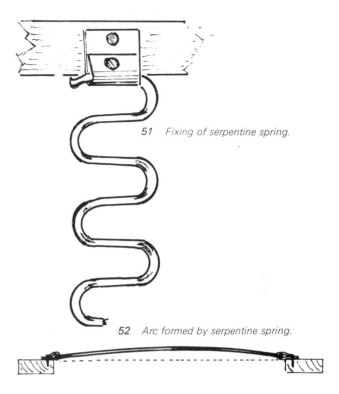

51   Fixing of serpentine spring.

52   Arc formed by serpentine spring.

53   Showing serpentine springing in back of easy chair.

Either the steel plate becomes detached from the frame because the head of the clout nail has broken, or the last bend or loop breaks away enabling the spring to release itself and curl back. These faults often result from a sudden overloading of the springs at a vital spot.

An emergency treatment where a length of spring has broken close to its fixing plate is to loop a length of upholstery webbing around the last two loops of the spring, apply strain to the webbing to bring the arc of the spring to its original position, then tack the webbing in approximately the same position as the fixing clip was.

The majority of upholstered easy chairs and settees are designed to accommodate seat and back cushions. Most of these are of single seat or back size (other than squab cushions which often are full width settee seat size), filled with various forms of soft fillings.

The border depth of seat cushions is normally 10 cm (4 in.), and of back cushions either 7.5 cm (3 in.) or 5 cm (2 in.).

The earliest cushions or pads were filled with lambswool or horsehair. Lambswool-filled squabs were used on such items as X chairs and farthingale chairs and were fairly bulky shapeless forms of cushioning. Later, the traditional squab was filled with horsehair contained in a hessian case stitched around the edge to retain its flatness and square sides (plate 19 on page 30). Feather and down filled cushions were a more recent development.

Feather and down filled cushions

A feather and down filled cushion is by far the most comfortable and durable, provided it is made correctly, and has a high proportion of down in it. Down, the light fluffy undercoating of waterfowl, is by far the softest and most resilient of the feather/down mixtures: a 100 per cent down filled cushion is very expensive but ultra-soft, and needs no shaking to return it to its original thickness after being sat on or leaned against. Eider down, from the eider duck, used in earlier cushion and bed cover (eiderdown) fillings, is now seldom used owing to its exorbitant cost. Poultry feathers, which have thick quills and are much coarser, have the least resilience. A much larger amount of them are needed, and they make a much rougher type of cushion, which has to be shaken up frequently to keep it plump. For a cushion filling which adds so much to the comfort of the seat, it is wise to use the best materials one can afford. The higher the price paid, the more down will be included in the mixture.

The feather/down filling should be placed in a waxed cambric interior case constructed with separate compartments to ensure the filling remains equal over the whole area throughout its life. The partitions forming the compartments should be machined between the top and bottom panels. On no account should the cambric interior case be omitted. If the feathers and down are put into the covering case only, in a very short time they will start to emerge until eventually there is little in the cushion.

First, using stout paper, make a template of the actual finished size and shape of the cushion fitting snugly up to the arms and back of the chair and flush with the front edge. Then on the template mark with pencil the lines along which the interior divisions or walls are to be machined. The top and bottom panels of the interior case should now be cut from cambric. If making one cushion only, lay the full width cambric folded so there are two layers, or, if making two cushions, lay another folded width on top so that you have four layers. Place the cushion template on to the layers of cambric, and pin it down to prevent it moving. Remember that the template is the size of the finished case, and the cambric should be cut larger to allow for seaming and the doming of the material when the case is filled. Approximately 2.5 cm (1 in.) oversize on all sides will suffice for most chair cushions. The same applies to settee cushions. The latter will usually be of a slightly different size from the easy chair cushions, whether it be a two or three seater settee, but if they are the same size they can all be cut together.

After cutting the panels with the surplus allowed all round, tap a pointed instrument through the template and layers of cambric close to the ends of the pencilled lines so that the material is punctured with small holes. As cambric is a very tightly woven fabric, the holes will remain whilst a pencil line is drawn across the fabric to indicate

where the interior partition walls are to be machined. Each panel can be done in turn as the marking holes will be in each piece.

Cut the interior walls of the casing from cambric, making them about 3.5 cm (1½ in.) deeper than the side borders are to be. The reason for this is that when the case is filled, the walls will not remain upright but become distorted with the pressure of the filling against them. Their greater depth will prevent the top and bottom panels from being pulled down and appearing concave. The ends of the partition walls should be tapered to the same depth as the borders. The walls can now be machined with the edges being folded over as they are machined. Figures 53 and 54 show two kinds of compartment systems. One has two interior walls across the width of it; the other has one inner wall across the width, and two running from back to front. This second system is a better arrangement than the former, but entails a little more work. It is necessary to fix the interior walls in position before the side borders have been sewn, as they cannot be put in afterwards.

53 Four compartment feather down cushion.
54 Three compartment feather down cushion.

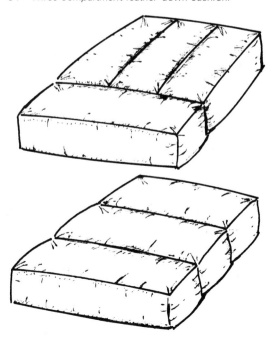

Now that the top and bottom panels are connected together by the partition walls, the outside border may be sewn around the edge of one of the panels. The cambric border should be cut 2 cm ($\frac{3}{4}$ in.) wider than the intended final depth of the finished cushion, preferably in one length if possible. If the available material is not sufficiently long to do this, shorter lengths may be joined provided the join is well machined with a small stitch using a french seaming or edge stitching. This should be done throughout as it helps to prevent the escape of feathers or down.

When the border has been sewn completely around one panel, the free ends of the interior walls, having previously been tapered to the width of the border, must be sewn to it in the appropriate places. The remaining panel must now be machined to the other edge of the border, and openings of approximately 4.25 to 4.50 cm (4 to 5 in.) left at the ends of the compartments for inserting the filling. Once the cushion has been filled, the openings may be machined or closed by hand sewing.

Where an original feather or down cushion is being retained, the case should be examined to ensure that it is still downproof. Should the cambric have deteriorated, it is a worthwhile investment to make a new case, even if only a plain one without compartments, to slip over the original to prevent the escape of the feathers or down. Also, many years of use may have broken the feather quills and reduced the bulk of the filling. If this has happened, carefully undo the stitching at one end of each compartment, and insert an additional mixture of feathers and down to restore the cushion to its original depth and quality.

The exterior covering may be cut from the same template as the inside case, but add 1 cm ($\frac{3}{8}$ in.) for seaming if the covering is to be finished with piping or a plain seam. If ruching is to be used as a trimming, no allowance should be made on the top and bottom panels for seaming, so that the ruche shows nicely without being jammed between the cushion edge and chair or settee arm. An allowance should however be made on the border.

To insert the interior filled case into its exterior covering, an opening should be left along one of the back edges. Once the inner case has been inserted, the opening should be slip-stitched. When removing an interior case from an old cushion for re-making this slip-stitching should be cut away. If the stitching was originally done well it may be difficult to see.

There are, of course, several other types of fillings used for cushions which have developed and been used over the years, many with a preformed type of interior designed to give a clean square edged appearance. Others are intended to simulate, at a lower cost, the feather filled cushion. Although these generally appear untidy, they are not objectionable to some, as they give an inviting look of comfort.

Interior sprung cushions

Two or three forms of these have been used in upholstery work from approximately 1930. The 'open coil' type of spring unit was incorporated in the wartime 'Utility' range of upholstered pieces. The open coil unit, encased in hessian with a wrap of linter felt, was a construction of convenience during a period of wartime restrictions and post war material shortages. Such a construction had a limited life because the open coil springs soon buckled and became noisy, and the cotton felt broke up. It is now obsolete, as other forms of interior are more convenient and easier to produce. As it is not practicable to remake or repair the original unit, it should be replaced with some other form of filling.

A better quality unit for a spring cushion is the pocketed type (figure 55). This has a number of small diameter cylindrical springs, each encased in fine muslin, clipped

55 *Pocketed spring interior cushion.*

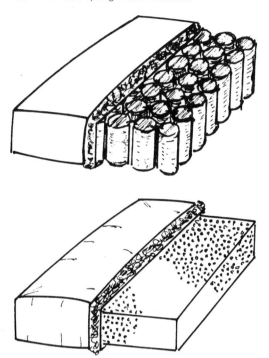

55 Pocketed spring interior cushion.

*56 Foam interior with crimped polyester fibre –
giving a simulated down cushion.*

together with 'hog rings' to form the cushion interior. This is a very durable unit, noiseless, with less chance of the filling being forced between and through the springs. Varying types of fillings are used over the pocketed unit, such as hair, cotton felt, rubberized hair, sheet kapok, etc. Whilst it is difficult to obtain a replacement spring, frequently it will be found that the original unit is still serviceable and re-usable.

Polyurethane and latex foam fillings

Polyurethane foam is probably the most widely used material for cushion interiors in present day upholstery. There is virtually no preparation involved other than cutting to size from the sheet. In some cases, even this is not necessary as the interiors can be supplied pre-cut to the required sizes by suppliers of the foam. Not only do the manufacturers supply cut cushion sizes but also fabricated shapes to designers' specifications for the mass production market.

There are a large number of different hardnesses of urethane foam available for upholstery, from high resistant to ultra soft. It is most important to use the most appropriate density and hardness for the work in hand. For seating purposes, a good quality high resistant foam should be used to withstand heavy loading, whereas for backs or back cushions, a much softer foam is suitable. Foam interiors should be cut about 2 cm ($\frac{3}{4}$ in.) larger than the finished size of the average chair seat cushion.

Figure 56 shows polyurethane foam and polyester crimped fibre used together to form a simulated feather cushion. A core of very soft foam is cut to a suitable size, a wrap of polyester fibre is placed around it, and the cover case is then drawn over. The polyester fibre fill may be used on its own without foam, but as it is expensive, it is more economical to use it in conjunction with foam. As the polyester fibre is very soft and bulky, it will be much larger than its case. Without the aid of mechanical compressers which are used in mass production, the home upholsterer will probably need a helper to achieve a successful result.

Reconstituted or chip foam (granulated off-cuts reformed into sheets), available in grades varying from medium to very hard, may be laminated with normal urethane foam to form numerous shapes. It is especially useful for walling purposes (plate 54): pieces 2.5 cm (1 in.) thick will give a firm edge which is often necessary when using the very soft foams.

Latex foam is a more costly product than urethane foam, but has greater resilience. Originally supplied in cavity sheet form, with a smooth surface and cavities on the underside, for the purpose of making cushions, nowadays it is also produced in a wide variety of moulded shapes to suit most requirements. Although latex cavity sheeting is now rarely used by upholstery manu-facturers for cushion making because less time consuming methods of production have been developed, the material is still available and useful to the home up-holsterer.

When making cushions from cavity sheeting, the cavities should be placed and stuck together, after the required shape has been cut with the aid of a template. The uneven sides which result from cutting through the cavities, should be covered by walls of 1.2 cm ($\frac{1}{2}$ in.) solid sheet latex. This must be stuck on each side and the front and back faces to give a smooth finish. It is to allow for the walling that the cushion shape

is cut fractionally smaller than it otherwise would have been. In any case, the interior should be a little larger than the finished cushion, to create a slight tension in the top covering which prevents it from wrinkling.

Latex foam deteriorates quickly if ex-posed to strong daylight or sunlight. In order to avoid this, an undercover of tightly woven cotton or linen cloth should be put on immediately over the latex. This will prevent any light filtering through the covering.

54 Use of reconstituted foam (chip foam). Reconstituted foam 2.5 cm (1″) stuck to outer edges to give firmer support to covering on edges.

SECTION FOUR

Upholstery Fabrics and Trimmings

TYPES OF FABRICS AVAILABLE

The most expensive item in refurbishing upholstery is the covering fabric. The choice of fabric is, therefore, very important and should be considered with some care. A number of fabrics on sale in departmental stores, purporting to be upholstery fabrics, are often unsuitable for this purpose, because they lack the abrasion resistance or 'body' necessary for a 'tight' upholstery covering as distinguished from a loose covering, which may be cotton or linen printed fabric, which is frequently laundered.

Where restoration of an antique piece is being undertaken, the correct type of covering for the particular period should be used. Most furniture periods had particular coverings associated with them with typical styles of motifs which were popular within a certain span of years. The restoration covering chart on pages 160 to 161 will be of some assistance in deciding on the correct covering and motif for the period piece.

Choosing an appropriate covering, estimating the length required, cutting and working the fabric require a certain amount of confidence. Both the amateur and professional upholsterer may become somewhat apprehensive when faced with ordering and cutting an expensive material. Mistakes can be costly, so this part of the work should be approached with caution but not trepidation. Before embarking on the covering stage it is as well to understand a few technical details about fabrics and their uses.

The usual width of upholstery fabrics is 122 cm (48 in.) to approximately 132 cm (52 in.). When estimating quantities it is advisable to assume that they are the narrower width. Certain fabrics, such as corduroys, velvets and printed linens, are sometimes produced in even narrower widths than these. Their widths can vary from 68.5 cm (27 in.) to 91.5 cm (36 in.). For tight covering of upholstery these narrower widths are usually uneconomical as they involve more wastage than the usual full width fabrics.

Plain woven fabrics consist of two sets of threads which interlace at right angles. In most fabrics there is a narrow band of a more firmly woven and stronger yarn along each edge known as the selvedge. The threads which run parallel with the selvedge (along the length of the material) are known as warp threads, and the threads running across the cloth (selvedge to selvedge) are known as weft threads (figure 57).

Designs on woven patterned fabrics may be produced either on Dobby or Jacquard looms. The Dobby loom produces cloth with small geometric patterns and a small 'repeat' using a limited number of 'healds' (i.e. frames raising the warp yarns). The Jacquard loom weaves very intricate and delicate patterns, using many coloured threads with a repeat of any desired length. Each movement of the shuttle across the warp threads is controlled by punched cards. Most delicate and decorative fabrics will have been Jacquard woven. Patterns on chintzes, cretonnes, etc., are applied by roller or screen printing after the fabric has been woven on a plain or 'tappet' loom. A pattern woven into a fabric will last as long as the fabric itself, whereas a pattern printed on a fabric may fade if subjected to sunlight.

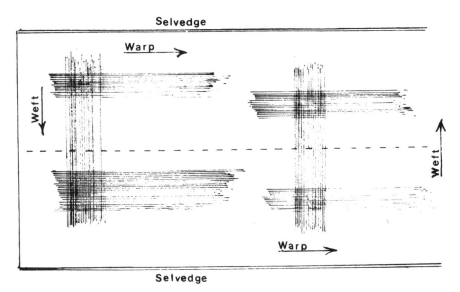

Selvedge

Warp →

Weft

Weft

← Warp

Selvedge

57   *The 'warp' and 'weft' of fabric.*

55   Moulded shell upholstered chair.

If the latter are used they should carry a British Standards Institute resistance to fading grade.

In recent years, knitted fabrics have been used extensively for covering the expanded polystyrene or rigid polyurethane moulded chairs used in contemporary upholstery design (plate 55). The majority of these moulded shells have compound curves which are incompatible with older style woven fabrics, developed for their durability and resistance to wear. Knitted fabric, which has a looped construction in the direction of the weft or warp, will stretch and easily conform to the curves of modern furniture without the tailoring necessary for traditional straight weave fabric. Generally, stretch fabric does not look so attractive on the more conventional stuffover piece of upholstery. Modern simulated leather coverings also have a knitted base construction, with an 'expanded' vinyl coating. This means they are more flexible and easier to apply than their original counterpart, the woven base P.V.C., whose rigidity can cause 'fullness' in certain circumstances.

TRADITIONAL WOVEN COVERINGS

Tapestry

This is a fabric usually woven with coarse, coloured yarn. It is available in heavy and light weights for upholstery purposes. The woven patterns are frequently reproductions of original hand woven tapestries. Medium to light weights are reasonably easy to work with, but the heavier qualities pose problems with pleating, machining, etc. Woven in traditional designs tapestry is suitable for early restoration upholstery. Contemporary tapestries are available with modern design motifs.

Handwoven embroidery

Stitched in *petit point* or *gros point*, these are generally embroidered with wool yarns, and often made to measure for particular items of upholstery. Edging pieces or an additional matching plain border are sometimes sewn to the panel of embroidery to enlarge it to fit the item, as the embroiderer often omits the last few rows of stitches which would ensure a comfortable fit. Before the embroidery is applied to the upholstery, it should be squared up. In most cases, the process of working the embroidery stitch by stitch tends to distort the base. This results in the finished panel being out of square and difficult to fix in place.

Velvet

Velvet is a 'pile' fabric originally made of silk yarn. Currently, many velvets are woven with a pile made from man-made fibres. The traditional method of using velvet on upholstered pieces is to have the brush of the pile running downward on inside and outside backs, downward on inside and outside arms, and forward on seats, so that the shading of the velvet is constant. However, in modern production, for economy's sake and to avoid joining the fabric, the practice is to run the brush of the pile sideways across the upholstered pieces, so that the shading of the material appears completely different when looked at from either side of the piece, or from each end of a settee.

Antique figured velvet with an indistinct pattern and a fine line running down its length is ideally suitable for restoration work, such as wing chairs, Knole settees, etc. Imported velvets were used on the earlier upholstered pieces.

Mohair or Utrecht velvet (plush) was popular during the Victorian period. It has a rather stiffer pile than conventional velvet, being made from the hair of the angora goat. As it is a form of wool fibre it is prone to attack by moth, and should be protected from this.

56 Box pouffe covered in leather and 'deep' buttoned. Finish is close nailed with brass nailing.

Upholstery damask

This is a light fabric, woven on a Jacquard loom with silk yarns. It has a fine intricate design usually incorporating a fairly large motif. As the background of the design is formed with a satin weave, the fabric is reversible; the design on the reverse side being in alternate shades to that on the face of the fabric. Silk damasks were popular for upholstery coverings, drapery and wall covering from the Adam period. Cotton damasks are available for upholstery coverings at a lower cost than the silk variety, but they are not so finely woven. Damask is susceptible to 'tack ties' if the covering is badly applied.

Brocade

A highly decorative fabric, brocade is Jacquard woven with small designs of many coloured silk yarns. The reverse of the fabric appears as striped weft-wise where the coloured yarns 'float' across, only appearing on the surface where these colours appear in the design. This is not a suitable fabric for heavy wear, only for light or occasional use. Brocade has been used for upholstery covering and drapery from the William and Mary period. At that time it was frequently imported from France by the yard, and later in individual set pieces for 'panel' upholstery.

Corduroy

A ribbed pile fabric with the ribs running in the direction of the warp (down the length of the cloth). Like velvet, it has a fine pile which will cause contrasting shading if applied with the brush of the pile in different directions. Corded fabrics were fashionable during the Victorian period, some having heavier corded ribs than the modern corduroys. The finer corduroys are still very popular.

Repp

A plain worsted or cotton fabric with fine ribs or lines running in the weft direction of the cloth. Better quality repps have a worsted face and are very hard wearing with high abrasion resistance. They are frequently used where a durable and soil-resisting cloth is necessary. The lower priced cotton versions are easier to work but not so durable.

Brocatelle

Said to be originally a copy of Italian tooled leather, this fabric has a raised pattern giving it an embossed appearance. Jacquard woven, the raised designs are formed from silk yarn in a satin weave. Qualities available vary considerably, the better grades being very durable and attractive.

Moquette

Moquette is a tough long wool pile fabric with a cotton ground. It is extremely hard-wearing, and is frequently used for transport seat covering. Moquette and uncut moquette are quite different in appearance and durability. Uncut moquette is a looped pile fabric with the loops formed from the warp yarns. It is easily snagged and damaged by the claws of domestic pets. Cats in particular are attracted to it and will pull the threads from the corners of a chair. This material should, therefore, be avoided by cat owners. Worsted uncut moquette is far more durable than its cotton counterpart.

A low priced cotton uncut moquette will quickly look shabby, the pile will flatten, and it will soil much more quickly than the worsted fabric.

Satin

This is a sheer lustrous material woven from silk yarn, generally difficult to work because of its fineness. Particularly if it is to be used for deep diamond buttoning, the silky nature of the fabric will prevent the pleats from laying flat in their correct positions. A fabric to be avoided for buttoning work. Slub satin is also a sheer fabric but with the surface broken up by the introduction of 'slubs' into the weft. Slubs are uneven places purposely spun into the yarn so that the surface of the woven fabric is uneven, and not so sheer as satin.

Chintz

Chintz is printed cotton, either glazed or unglazed, first used during the William and Mary period. It is suitable only for occasional use on such items as bedroom chairs, dressing table coverings, and curtaining.

Printed linen

This is plain woven linen with various designs printed on the surface. First used in the early and late Jacobean periods with overall floral entwined patterns and acanthus leaf designs, it is suited to loose cover work owing to its non-fraying properties.

Folkweave fabric

Folkweave is a cotton fabric, loosely woven with coarse yarns. Because of the number of long warp float yarns (yarns which carry over the surface for some distance before returning into the weave) which are easily snagged, this material is generally unsuitable for tight or loose covering of upholstery. It should be used only for curtaining.

MODERN COVERINGS

It is necessary to be rather more selective in the choosing of a fabric made from man-made fibres for upholstery than in choosing a traditional type of material. There are some which are not suitable; some do not have the 'body' or weight suitable for the tight covering of upholstery, and some when stretched over will allow the base to show through the weave of the cloth. Glass fibre fabrics should on no account be used; whilst suitable for curtaining, they would have a relatively short life as upholstery covering, with the added risk of irritation to the skin.

A large number of upholstery fabrics utilising man-made fibres of the same type often have different trade names, particularly so in different countries of origin. Nylon, for example, is produced under many trade names. Some fabrics utilising man-made fibres which are well known and generally readily obtainable, and suitable as upholstery covering, are: viscose rayon, nylon, acrylic and polyester.

Viscose rayon

This is probably the cheapest and most widely used material; often the fabric comprises rayon yarn mixed or blended with cotton or linen yarns. This gives satisfactory wear if used in suitable weights. Rayon Damask is attractive and reliable in wear. Rayon fibres are used in other types of cloth, some textured surface weaves, others with a coarse and loose weave. It is generally easy to work with.

Names in the rayon fibre field are: Fibro, Sarille, Evlan, Vincel.

Nylon

There is probably a greater variety of types of fabrics produced using nylon fibre than any other, some being suitable for upholstery covering whilst others are not, due to their light weight. A number of 'nap' fabrics (velvet types) with long or short pile are made from nylon. These generally are hard wearing having a high abrasion resistance, although the deep plush types tend to matt after a period.

For the covering of the polystyrene-shell type of easy chair, a nylon laminated fabric is advisable. These fabrics are constructed with a fine nylon 'pile' (similar to velveteen) with a thin sandwich of foam on a knitted base. The advantage of this type of fabric is that it readily stretches, so it is easier to get it to conform to the compound curves of the moulded chair shape.

The majority of mass-produced off-the-peg loose covers use a completely knitted construction using nylon yarn. This is unsuitable for use as tight covering or permanent covering because it has far too much stretch; the yarn would open too much and it would also ladder when cut.

Names in the nylon field are: Bri-nylon, Autron, Celon, Perlon, Enkalon.

Acrylic

Fabrics made from acrylic fibres have become very popular in recent years. Dralon velvet is most extensively used because of its versatility; it is made in a variety of qualities, and its colours are most attractive. One of its chief advantages is its ability to be lightly sponged to remove light stains. In addition to velvets, many other types of fabric are produced using acrylic yarn – they can generally be used with confidence.

Names in the acrylic field are: Acrilan, Dralon, Courtelle, Orlon, Teklon.

Polyester

There are not so many polyester fabrics suitable for upholstery as the other synthetics, as the cloth tends to be too light weight. Where upholstery cloth is obtainable it is usually of mixed fibre content.

Names in the polyester field are: Terylene, Terlenka, Tergal.

SELECTING, PREPARING AND CUTTING THE COVERING

Choosing the fabric

When selecting a decorative figured fabric for the covering, consider the pattern repeat, that is, the distance between the beginning of one motif on the fabric and the beginning of the next. With smaller motifs, the repeat may be quite small, perhaps about 22.5 cm (9 in.), causing little problem in the cutting. A motif may, however, be very large: up to 94 cm (37 in.). Where there is a large repeat, the appearance of the finished work will be spoilt if the covering has been cut or positioned badly, so that the motifs are not lying centrally on chair seats or backs, or are too low or too high.

Unless the work requires a fabric with a large repeat, use a smaller patterned fabric. This will result in less wastage in cutting, and make for easier planning. Figure 58 shows an easy chair with motifs correctly positioned. Where fabric incorporating a central motif is used to cover a suite, or a number of chairs, all the coverings should appear identical with the patterns situated in exactly the same positions on each piece.

Upholstery fabric with large single floral panels on each half width is obtainable with a matching plain fabric. The motif on each panel is about 43 cm (17 in.) deep with an adequate amount of surrounding plain weave around and between each motif. The panels are suitable for seats or seat cushions, and the remainder of the upholstery can be covered in the matching plain fabric.

Alternatively both seat and back cushions could be panelled. This treatment is usually most effective for traditional styles.

Planning the layout

The professional upholsterer generally works in a set sequence; completely covering the arms, the seat, back and outsides in turn, before going on to the next stage. Where only restoration work is being undertaken, some of the upholstery may already be in position. This often makes the locating and cutting of stiles more difficult, but despite this, it is prudent when working from a bare frame to first stuff and complete in calico before measuring for covering.

If the original top covering has been removed in reasonable condition, the various pieces can be used as templates for cutting the new fabric. Any distortion which may have taken place whilst the cover was in its original position must be smoothed and straightened out, particularly if the covering is from a deeply buttoned piece.

58 *Positioning of motifs. Patterns on fabric should be shown to advantage.*

Before attempting to cut the fabric, work out on paper a small scale cutting plan. In fact, it is wise to do this much earlier on to avoid over-estimating the amount of fabric required. Figures 59 to 61 give examples of cutting plans, and specify the items the covering is being cut for. Obviously, it would be impossible to produce in this book cutting plans for every style and shape, but these examples give an idea of the general procedure. Despite any saving of fabric that may be effected by turning the pieces around on the cutting plan, the pattern should always be set the correct way on each part and should 'follow through'. Failure to observe this principle will result in an unsightly covering, particularly those with a floral pattern, which usually has one way of placing only.

Upholstery cloth comes either in full width rolls, or first folded in half then rolled. The pattern is generally woven so that the two half widths of the cloth are identical (irrespective of the length of the repeat along the cloth), and in many cases the centre of the full width of the fabric will have the same pattern. Wherever possible, full use should be made of half width cuts for easy chair seats and backs so that the patterns can be centred (figure 62). For settees with a similar pattern, use the full width, as this is the most economical method of cutting. There are instances where a half width is just a little too narrow. This difficulty can be overcome by machining a strip of the fabric along each side edge or for whatever shorter distance is required.

59   Cutting plan: Bordered arm easy chair.

53" 135.0cm			15" 38.0cm	12" 30.5	6½" 16.5cm	10" 25.5cm	23" 58.5cm.	10" 25.5cm	19" 48.0cm	19" 48.0cm

Arm border. | Back facing. | join. | join.

join I.A. | join bdr.

| Outside arm. | Outside arm. | Inside back. | Seat lip. | Seat border. | Cushion base. | | Inside arm. | Inside arm. |

Half width

join. | join. | Cushion borders. | join.

Cushion top. | Bias lining | Outside back.

join I.A. | join bdr.

Arm border | Back facing.

COVER PLAN.

Covering required 425.5 c.m. (4⅔ yards.)

With lining seat Platform.

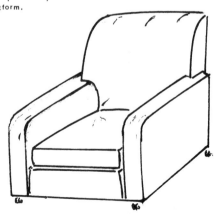

Often this is not noticeable. If the easy chair seat or back is extra wide and it is not practicable to add joining pieces, it will be necessary to make the cuts from the centre of the full width. Utilize, if possible, the surplus cut from each side on another part of the work, as in figure 59. One must accept that in the cutting of fabric for an upholstered piece a certain amount of wastage is inevitable. How much will depend upon the sizes and shapes of the cuts. The off-cuts can be used to make various items for the home.

Cutting the covering

Cutting of the covering must be done with considerable care. Wherever possible, all the pieces should be cut at the one time, rather than at different stages in the progress of the work. First unroll and check that the fabric is the required length, as suppliers usually refuse to exchange material once it has been cut into. Look for flaws in the weave, and if one is apparent, arrange the cutting so that the flaw is either missed and cut out, or so that it is in a less noticeable place. Spread the fabric out on as large a flat surface as possible and, referring to the cutting plan which has already been worked out, mark out the covering with tailor's chalk remembering that this chalk is difficult to remove. If there is any likelihood of the marking being incorrect, use ordinary white chalk which will easily rub off. As each part is marked out and cut, write its initials on the reverse side, and when applying the covering to the job check the initials to ensure that the correct piece is being used. Without this guide, it is easy to use an outside back for the inside back, or an inside back for the seat. Figure 63 gives the names of various parts of the covering.

23" 58.5 c.m.	18" 46.0 c.m.	36" 91.5 cm.	22" 56.0 c.m.	5" 12.5 cm.	23" 58.5 c.m.	19" 48.0 c.m.
Inside arm	Outside arm	Outside back	Cushion bottom	Cushion border	Outside wing / Inside wings	facing / 28.0 c.m. / 26.0 cm / Front lip / Cushion borders
Inside arm	Outside arm	Inside back	Cushion top	Cushion border	Outside wing	facing

COVER PLAN.
Covering required 371 cm (4¼ yards)
With uncovered tension sprung seat.

60 Cutting plan: Wing easy chair.

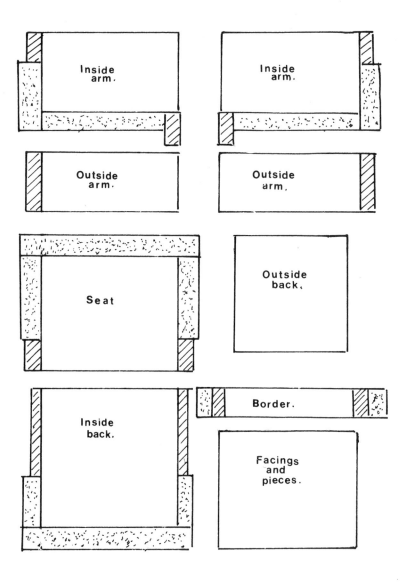

Inside arm.

Inside arm.

Outside arm.

Outside arm.

Seat

Outside back.

Inside back.

Border.

Facings and pieces.

 Represents joined cover pieces.

 Represents hessian flys.

61 *Preparation of covering.*

62 *Centring of pattern on seat. Showing flys and spring edge pieces in position. Pattern should be slightly forward of centre.*

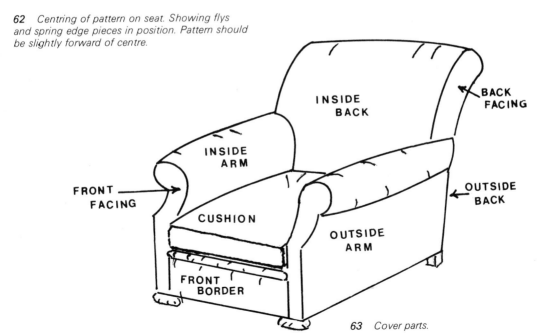

63 *Cover parts.*

UPHOLSTERY TRIMMINGS

Trimmings of various kinds are used on upholstered work to give decorative effects. Figure 64 shows a number of examples. In the past, craftsmen doing traditional upholstery work accepted that the seams of outside coverings and the edge seams on cushions should be hidden by a ruche or braid; also that the base edges of chairs or settees would be covered by some form of fringe or braid. Designers of modern upholstery, however, take the opposite view, and frequently leave all seams and bases without trimming to preserve the clean tailored appearance of the work.

The trimmings for upholstery work should be more substantial than those used for lampshades or general drapery. They should have a firm 'body' to them and be made from a cotton, silk, or perhaps, where the covering is wool, an all wool yarn. The types of trimmings used are listed below.

Braids

These are usually tightly woven with straight edges, and are referred to by the textile trade as narrow fabrics. They come in widths varying from approximately 0.6 cm ($\frac{1}{4}$ in.) to 3.6 cm ($1\frac{1}{2}$ in.). Braids are normally sewn to the covering using a circular needle, or, alternatively, the narrower widths may be glued in position.

Gimps

These usually have a looser and more unevenly woven decorative edge than braids. The method of attachment may be either with adhesive or with gimp pins. The loose threads of the gimp are opened to allow the pin to be hammered home and then covered by replacing the threads.

Ruches

There are a number of different types of upholstery ruches used to camouflage seams of cushions and joins in the outside backs, arms and wings of chairs. Ruches have a tightly woven flange which is either machined into the seam of a cushion covering, or tacked in position if used as a trimming on the frame.

Fringes

Fringes are generally used to decorate the base edges of upholstered work, but in some instances they are used elsewhere, for example, across the backs of Knole settees. Produced in many fancy forms, they are sewn in position with a circular needle. Fringes should be adjusted for height to allow for clearance of the floor covering, such as a carpet with deep pile.

Gimps

64 Upholstery trimmings.

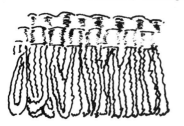

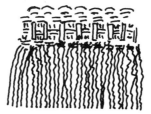

Ruches

Historical introduction

Leathers of various kinds and in varying finishes have enjoyed popularity as upholstery coverings over a great number of years. Because of its size and durability cow-hide has always been in demand. Other skins have, however, achieved great popularity at certain periods in our history.

Morocco, imported from Europe and Persia, and dyed in beautiful shades of blue, red, green and brown, was, from the latter part of the eighteenth century, used a good deal as a high quality chair covering. Being the skin from a species of mountain goat, it is a good deal smaller than the more usual cow-hide. An average cow-hide is approximately six times larger than a morocco skin. Consequently, the uses of morocco are far more limited. For larger work, it needs to be joined, or the work must be planned to suit the smaller size skin. In recent years the use of morocco has gradually declined because of its cost – it is far more expensive than cow-hide – and it is fragile – great care should be taken when working with it, as it can be stained by perspiration from the hands. Other than for prestige work, where expense is a minor factor, very little morocco is used now.

When using a number of skins, prior to cutting the skins which are to be used adjacent to each other, these should be shaded because of possible slight variations in dyeing.

There have also been various fashions in leather finishes. One of the earliest was a morocco-grained hide to simulate what was considered to be a more superior covering. These hides were stained with colours similar to morocco skins. After the 1914–18 war, reproduction leather upholstery became popular. Upholstery was covered in hide which was termed a 'first stained hide', that is, the finish was incomplete. The hide was then sprayed after covering with an antique colouring to reproduce a faded effect. The backs of settees and chairs at this time often carried embossed medallions or some form of floral design.

Attempts have been made to simulate leather for upholstery covering for very many years, the earliest being the so-called 'American cloth'. Introduced during the Victorian era, this was a fairly heavy covering with an impervious surface and a heavy cotton or duck base. The surface could be finished in many colours. This was followed by a similar but lighter type of imitation leather with the trade name of Rexine. Both were very popular in their day as they brought the look of leather to poorer homes, and had the added advantage that the sur-

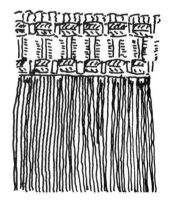

Fringes

face could be wiped clean with a damp cloth. Both of these materials were very difficult to work, particularly in cold weather when they were stiff and unpliable.

These were superseded soon after the 1939–1945 War by P.V.C. (poly-vinyl-chloride), with its plasticized surface coating on a plain woven cotton ground. This material had greater flexibility and greater pliability in cold weather than previous simulated leathers. It also had a greater variety of finishes to copy the graining of leather and other patterns. A further improvement came in the form of expanded P.V.C., which has its plasticized surface 'aerated' to enable it to expand and contract with its base. The latter, being constructed in a looped or knitted formation, has far more elasticity than a straight woven base cloth. Expanded vinyl is ideal for foam upholstery covering where the 'leather look' is required, because it does not need to be tensioned to retain its smoothness as do traditional woven coverings.

Polyurethane coated fabric has now been added to the range of simulated leathers. This gives the appearance of a fine, soft glove leather. The polyurethane coating is applied to a plain woven back cloth, so does not have quite the flexibility of expanded vinyl, but has a very attractive appearance.

Despite these developments, and the changes of fashion in furnishing, leather continues to have a place in home, boardroom and office. Both amateur and professional upholsterer can derive a great deal of satisfaction in working with leather. With modern finishes and processing methods skins available today are so soft and supple that they can be worked almost as easily as a soft fabric. The skins used many years ago were generally much thicker, tougher and more difficult to manage.

65 A cowhide. Approximate size of an average skin.

Obtaining and selecting the skins

One difficulty which may be encountered in using leather for small upholstered items, is finding a source of supply. Generally, curriers (processors of leather) are not keen on selling leather in quantities of less than a half skin, that is, a full skin cut lengthwise down the back bone. This is understandable as a skin, particularly one of a special colour, with a small piece cut from it, may be left on their hands. However, it is sometimes possible to find a leather user with a number of offcuts to dispose of.

Both leather and morocco are sold by the square measurement and not by the metre as fabric is. An average size skin would be 4.47 to 4.65 sq. metres (48 to 50 sq. ft). When a skin is purchased every part is measured, even to the small extremities which will obviously be waste (figure 65). Smaller or larger skins ranging from about 3.72 to 6.51 sq. metres (40 to 70 sq. ft) are obtainable, but it is not always possible to purchase the exact size skin required, so it is often necessary to accept the nearest size available.

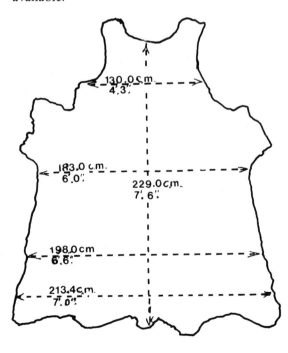

Because of the asymmetrical shape of a hide and the very uneven outer edges, there is always some unavoidable waste when cutting. There may also be certain marks, such as bad scars and abrasions, or even holes in the skin, which may have to be cut around. The amount of good usable leather from one particular size skin cannot, therefore, be guaranteed.

Unlike hide, simulated leather cloths are purchased by the metre or yard rather than by square measurement. Consequently, it is rather easier to estimate quantities needed, as there is not the problem of wastage to consider.

In estimating the quantity of leather needed for a particular upholstered piece, a percentage for wastage must be added to the net amount calculated. The amount of wastage in cutting will vary with the quality of the hide and the size of the pieces being cut. Wastage of leather from smaller cuts will be less than that from larger ones which are sometimes more difficult to place. As a general rule, for small cuts (loose seat covers) add 25 per cent for wastage on to the net amount calculated; allow an extra $33\frac{1}{3}$ per cent for medium cuts (fireside chair, small easy chair parts); and add 40 per cent for larger cuts. Failure to add these percentages for wastage on to the net calculation may result in having insufficient leather to complete a piece.

Planning the layout

Since cow-hide is a natural product and not man-made, small blemishes may be visible on parts of the hide. These natural marks may be scars from brambles or barbed wire, holes from warble fly burrowings (usually around the back bone area), or creases from folds in the skin (around the shoulder area). These imperfections, which in no way affect the wearing properties of the leather are its hallmark. As they are not found on substitutes, their presence proves beyond doubt that the material is genuine cow-hide.

Where occasionally a blemish is too much of an eyesore then it is necessary to cut round it, or to place it on the finished item where it will not be too noticeable.

The skin should be opened out and laid flat so that any really bad spots or weals can be seen at once. The area each side of the back bone (the centre of the skin down its length) is usually the most stable and cleanest part, and will work best. The extreme outer edges of the skin will often be 'papery', that is, very stretchy with the surface of the leather opening when stretched and revealing the interior fleshy fibres. These parts should be avoided if possible or, if they must be used, should be arranged so that they lie out of sight on the work. Templates should be cut for each part of the chair or settee to be covered, and laid upon the surface of the hide all together. Although they may be manoeuvred to get full value from the skin, it is better to lay them on squarely than at all angles to save a few inches. Where a large number of pieces are being cut from the same template, it is more convenient to make the templates from clear perspex so that any bad faults in the leather can be seen through the template before cutting. If paper or card templates are used, they have to be raised frequently so that the condition of the skin underneath them can be seen. Once the patterns have been suitably positioned, they should be chalked around with ordinary blackboard chalk, which will wipe away quite easily. Tailor's chalk should not be used because it is wax and cannot be removed if an error is made.

Cutting, machining and finishing

The cutting of leather and simulated leather is an operation which should be carefully thought out as it requires a good deal of skill. In a factory, a good cutter can save his firm a good deal of money in the course of a year. Make as much use as possible of 'flys' when planning the cutting of leather (and of other fabrics too for that matter) as these will cut down the amount of covering material needed. Flys are used wherever possible on most upholstered work. The fly consists of a suitable width strip of hessian or any strongly woven material, machined along the bottom edge of an arm or the side and back edges of a seat covering, and used in many other instances. The covering should be cut to a size just sufficient to allow the fly to be beyond the sight line, or where the covering disappears from sight, so that tacking takes place on the strip of 'fly' (figures 61 and 62).

Leather and simulated leathers should be machined with a large stitch to avoid perforating the covering too closely and causing it to split at the machine line.

The final finishing of leather and simulated leather upholstered pieces differs from that of soft fabric covered work because the slip-stitching method used normally for soft covers is not suitable for leather work. Various types of fancy nails, either spaced some distance apart or close together may be used (plate 56). Covered studs may be used but this involves matching ready-made studs to the upholstery leather or having them specially made from the leather being used for the rest of the job.

A good deal of earlier leather work was finished with leather covered lead moulding which had fixing pins embedded in the lead body of the moulding at approximately 10 cm (4 in.) intervals. These were very carefully hammered with a leather-headed mallet close into the polished rebate where the covering had been gimp pinned (figure 66).

Whilst this type of finish is still used, the making and application of it is carried out by only a limited number of craftsmen, and unfortunately it is very expensive. A modern substitute, covered in P.V.C. only, is available and used frequently but this does not have the superior finish of lead moulding.

As leather upholstery is costly in terms of money and labour, it is wise to protect it by feeding the leather and replacing the natural oils which will dry out in a very hot or centrally heated atmosphere. Proprietary brands of hide foods are available, and they should occasionally be rubbed into the leather to help to preserve its appearance. Never use wax furniture polish or aerosol polish sprays on leather as they will clog the pores and produce white patches. Once the wax has built up, it is impossible to remove without danger of damaging the leather.

66   Leather-covered lead moulding.

1   Day bed restored and covered in watered silk with velvet stripes

2   Drop-end settee re-upholstered and covered in tapestry

3 Victorian wing easy chair restored and covered in leather

SECTION FIVE

Advanced Repairs and Restoration

UPHOLSTERY BUTTONING

Introduction and preparation

Buttoning was originally used on upholstery to assist in the shaping of fillings so that these conformed to the concave shapes of chair and settee backs and arms. It then became popular as an aid to decoration rather than construction, and was subsequently frequently used on flat surfaces such as wall panelling, coach trimming, etc. Buttoning has remained popular to this day, not only on the traditional type of work but also with contemporary designs.

'Float' buttoning is frequently used in upholstery in place of deep buttoning. The former is suitable for work with a shallower depth of upholstery. The buttons are pulled down only slightly so that their surfaces are only a little below the upholstered surface. This is a simpler method of applying button decoration, omitting the diamond shaped pleating between the buttons. Whilst float buttoning is normally used for decorative purposes only, there may be instances where it can be incorporated in the shaping of upholstery to eliminate 'fullness' or wrinkling in covering which would otherwise be difficult to avoid (figure 67).

67 Float buttoning. Used to retain concave shape of seat.

Deep diamond buttoning of upholstery is highly skilled work if carried out by traditional methods. Some years of practice are needed to enable one to tackle confidently any type of buttoned job. A particularly large or difficult job, such as a Chesterfield settee, should not be undertaken without previous experience of smaller buttoned work, so that some appreciation of the problems and difficulties one is likely to encounter can be gained. Deep diamond buttoning in leather is much more difficult than using soft fabric.

For the success of deep diamond buttoning, preparation is most important. The measuring must be accurate, as must the marking of the covering to allow the correct amount of fullness for the pleating which forms the diamonds. Because there are very many different styles of buttoned chairs, settees, etc., it is impossible to give detailed instructions for dealing with each one. The basic principles of deep buttoning, set out below, can be used in the majority of jobs one may come across. Since this book is primarily intended as an aid to repair and renovation work, it is assumed that most readers will be dealing with re-upholstery and that the basic construction will be in place.

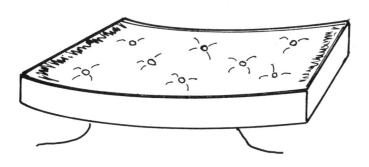

Before stripping off the old covering and filling, always make a detailed sketch of the original work. Measure exactly the position of the original buttons; distances from the tops of backs and fronts of seats; the spacing between buttons back to front, and side to side; the depth the buttons were sunk into the filling from the top surface of the upholstery; and, particularly important, the depth of the seat, from its front edge to where the base of the back touches it. Once these measurements have been recorded, the original covering should be removed carefully as it is invaluable for re-marking the new fabric. Note that the groundwork measurements (the distances between the buttons on the base) are less than those on the covering. This is to give the covering sufficient fullness for pleating between the buttons. If the hessian, scrim, stitching, etc., is dilapidated enough to need replacing, note carefully where the buttons were stitched on the hessian, as the latter must be replaced in exactly the same position.

If new buttoning is planned, or the positions of existing buttons are to be changed, a good method of deciding the most suitable arrangement for the new buttoning is to place a tack through the hessian in each proposed button position to represent a button. The tacks can then be changed round until a suitable arrangement has been arrived at, their positions marked with tailor's chalk on both sides of the hessian, and the tacks removed.

The diamond shapes will vary according to the size and shape of the piece being worked. 'Square' diamonds (the same measurements down and across) are more suitable for squarer seats and backs, whereas the 'long' diamonds (longer down than across) are suitable where the upholstery tends to be long and narrow. Diamond shapes should not be too small. When planning, remember these diamond sizes will generally appear much smaller when completed with the covering in position than they appear on the groundwork. Anything

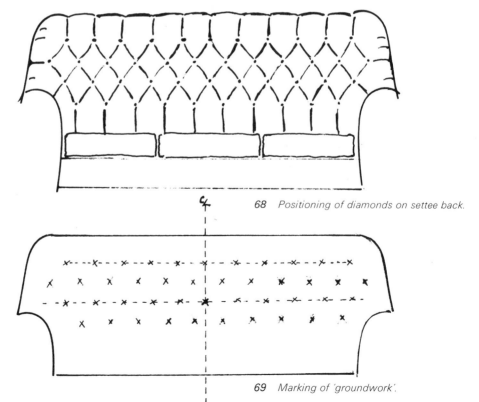

68 *Positioning of diamonds on settee back.*

69 *Marking of 'groundwork'.*

less than 10 cm (4 in.) between buttons will look overcrowded, and be difficult to work. The ideal is an uncrowded and nicely shaped series of diamonds to suit the area on which they are situated.

To achieve a balanced appearance, the positioning of the outer rows of buttons on arms, back, etc., should be as near as possible half the width of the diamond on the groundwork. For example, if the widths of the diamonds across a seat are 12.5 cm (5 in.), the outer rows should be 6.25 cm ($2\frac{1}{2}$ in.) from the sides of the seat. Similarly with a back: if the diamonds are 15 cm (6 in.) deep, the top row should be 7.5 cm (3 in.) from the top edge of the back (figure 68). Generally, the bottom row of buttons on a back will appear better if the distance is rather more than that of a full diamond from the surface of the seat, or, if it is a cushion seat, from the top surface of the cushion (figure 69).

The amount of fullness to be given to the fabric when marking for a normal depth of buttoning should be approximately one fifth more than the groundwork measurements, for example, for a diamond 15 cm by 17.5 cm (6 in. by 7 in.), the covering marking should be 18 cm by 21 cm ($7\frac{1}{8}$ in. by $8\frac{5}{16}$ in.). These figures are suitable for flat buttoned surfaces but must be adjusted for curved surfaces. For example, over the radius of the scroll back or arm of a Chesterfield, additional material should be given for the greater distance the covering will have to take around the curve. Conversely, a concave buttoned surface will require a smaller amount of fullness to avoid the formation of an area of slack material between the buttons which will be impossible to remove.

The 'stretchability' of the covering fabric must also be considered when calculating the fullness to allow for buttoning. Some fabrics will stretch more across the width than the length, or even stretch a good deal both ways more than average. Where it is obvious that there will be a certain amount of extension during the working of the material, the amount of fullness should be reduced when marking the button positions on the covering. If in doubt, a good idea of the fullness required can be established by measuring between the groundwork button points with a tape measure allowing it to loop up to the radius that the covering and filling will take. It may be that at one point one amount of fullness will be required, and at another point this may have to be varied on the same piece of covering.

Marking button positions on the covering should always be done on the reverse side; a wrong position marked with tailor's chalk on the surface will be difficult to remove and may damage the fabric in the process.

For larger areas of buttoning, such as longer settees or couches, or perhaps wide headboards, the usual covering fabric will not be sufficiently wide or a piece of leather may not be long enough. This is frequently the case when using small skins such as moroccos. Joins should be made in the material so that they are hidden under the diamond pleating. This is called 'vandyking', figures 70 and 71 show the method of marking the covering fabric or leather for the vandyked join.

If working with fabric the join may be machined, but hand sewing is necessary with leather, as machining tends to distort the shapes cut between the button points. This will cause puckering and wrinkling which will be difficult to remove when making the pleats and result in visible joining lines. If done carefully and correctly two, or even more, joins may be made on a long buttoned seat or back without any visible sign.

Figure 72 illustrates different types of buttons normally used in upholstery production. It is possible to recover an old button with a new piece of fabric but this tends to be rather bulky on the back where the fabric is drawn together, and prevents

70 *Marking of covering. Showing vandyked join in covering.*

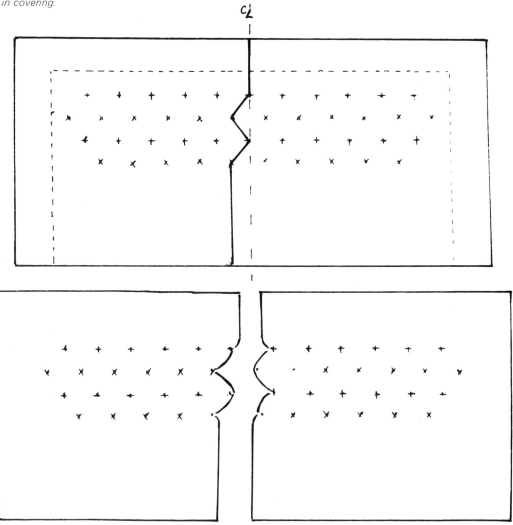

c↓
L

71 *Showing material cut to make vandyked join.*

the button from sinking into its bed snugly. It is wise to have new buttons made professionally from your own material if possible. The backs of some machine-made buttons will have a pad of fabric through which the twine is threaded with a 'buttoning' needle, or alternatively, a wire loop will be on the back of the button to thread the twine through. Of the two types, the soft pad back is the better as it allows the button to be pulled up very tightly into its 'bed', whereas the wire loop tends to restrict the

pulling down process, often leaving the button standing somewhat proud from the surface. A proprietary brand of D.I.Y. button moulds for making buttons of various sizes is obtainable from departmental or drapery stores. Whilst these buttons are suitable for certain light applications they are not really sturdy enough to withstand the strain incurred in forming the cover pleating characteristic of deep buttoning.

To fix the buttons in position a fine upholstery buttoning needle should be used
rather than a thicker needle which may
wrench the tuft out from the back of the
tufted back buttons. With float buttoning,
the buttons are better tied-off from the
base hessian. A scrap of hessian or webbing
should be tucked into the loop of twine
before the slip-knot is pulled tight. This is
generally referred to as a 'butterfly', its
purpose being to prevent the twine from
pulling through the hessian and releasing
the button, either whilst being worked, or
at a later stage when the hessian has
deteriorated.

72   Different types of upholstery buttons.

Restoration of buttoned chair in leather

American cloth (early simulated leather) was the original covering on the heavily carved and turned chair shown in plate 57. The thickly padded chair seat is detachable. The seat frame is held in position by means of a dowel peg protruding from the top edge of the front seat rail, locating with a hole in the corresponding position on the seat frame.

Whilst the upholstered back panel is in reasonable condition (plate 58), it is necessary to strip off the back completely in order to renew the outside back covering which is tacked in the rebate on the face of the back. In many instances backs of this type have a rebate on the back surface of the back frame so that the outside back may be tacked on after the inside has been fixed, so it is not always necessary to strip this completely before re-covering. Webbing and hessian on the seat has deteriorated and broken, and needs to be completely stripped and replaced. Plate 59 shows the chair frame stripped of all upholstery with the loose seat replaced in position. As shown in figure 73 the seat has triangular fillets fixed to the side and back upper surfaces, the front rail being left flat to allow greater depth of filling.

The seat should be upholstered off the job on a flat bench top using three by three webbing, with a good quality hessian over; 1.2 cm ($\frac{1}{2}$ in.) improved tacks should be used on both. The original filling was a good quality horsehair usual in this type of chair. With a good teasing the hair is re-usable. A pad should be made across the front edge of the seat to the height of the side fillets

58 Showing back panel which has to be stripped to renew outside back.

59 Chair completely stripped showing rebate of back and seat frame.

57 Buttoned seat and panel back small chair to be restored.

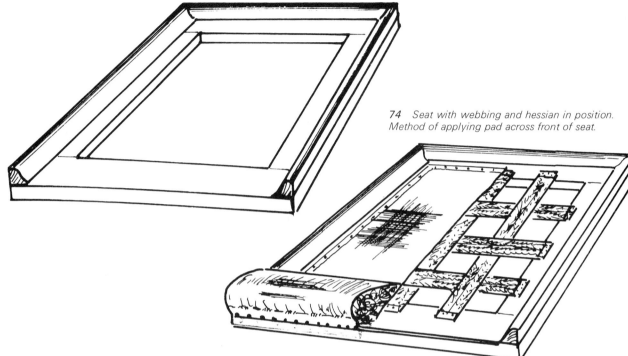

73 *Seat frame with fillets fixed to sides and back.*

74 *Seat with webbing and hessian in position. Method of applying pad across front of seat.*

(figure 74). The pad should be made by sewing with twine a strip of hessian or scrim approximately 15 cm (6 in.) wide to the hessian 10 cm (4 in.) back from the front edge. This should be stuffed with hair, and the hessian or scrim tacked down to the top corner edge of the front rail using 1 cm ($\frac{3}{8}$ in.) improved tacks. A blind-stitch should be made along the base of the pad against the rail to bring the filling forward and to consolidate the edge, as the leather will need a firm base to be strained against. With the pad in position and blind-stitched only, the hair filling can be inserted under bridle ties sewn into the hessian. The hair filling should be fairly dense in this case for leather covering, with the depth being rather greater than the side and back rails and front edge.

A covering of scrim should be applied over the hair, taken over the side and back rails and front edge, then tacked off with 1 cm ($\frac{3}{8}$ in.) improved tacks, after temporary tacking and running twine stuffing ties

through the scrim and base hessian. No further stitching is required other than the blind-stitch previously put into the front pad, as the side and back fillets provide the firm edge necessary for the 'cleaning' out of the leather.

The button positions on the groundwork scrim should now be planned. Having retained the old covering or taken measurements of the button spacings, this is quite a simple operation, but it must be done accurately. Plate 60 shows clearly the arrangement of the buttons before the chair was stripped. The measurement across the front of the seat is 45 cm (18 in.) so the three buttons across are 15 cm (6 in.) apart, and the two side buttons 7.5 cm (3 in.) in from the side edges. The depth of the seat (back to front) is 40 cm (16 in.) so the button spacing can be the same both ways, allowing the back row to be 10 cm (4 in.) from the back edge which is a little wider than the

60 Original condition of buttoned chair seat.

first row from the front edge. This allows for the back projecting and gives a balanced appearance. Buttoning and floral motifs should always be placed slightly forward of centre.

At this stage the leather for the seats should be cut to size, marked and creased in the appropriate places (figure 75). Care should be taken not to crease the leather wrongly as a crease in the wrong position cannot be eradicated. When cutting the leather to size be sure to allow sufficient for the fullness between the buttons, and for tacking to the underside of the frame.

The same button arrangement as marked on the seat should be marked on the underside of the leather, plus the allowance for fullness as described earlier on page 99. Wherever pleating between buttons, or from a side button to the side of the seat occurs, the leather should be creased, folded face to face, and hammered lightly on the

wrong side. This is to enable the pleats between the buttons to fold easily and lie flat. If this process is omitted, the pleats will tend to 'roll', and stand proud. Punch holes in the leather at the button positions to allow the needle to pass easily through. Should the leather be thin, or if morocco is being used, a small square of reinforcing linen 1.2 cm by 1.2 cm ($\frac{1}{2}$ in. by $\frac{1}{2}$ in.) should be pasted on the underside where the twine will be passing through the leather.

Lengths of twine should be cut and run through the scrim and hessian base, and back again, so there are two ends out of the top surface at each of the button positions. A 'second' filling of hair should now be applied over the scrim ensuring that the twines remain upright through the hair. A generous covering of cotton wadding is now laid over the hair: if skin wadding is being used three layers are advisable. Make small holes through the layers of wadding to pass the twines through, so that they all lie on the surface of the wadding.

Starting with the buttons of the centre diamond, and using a 20 cm or 25 cm (8 in. or 10 in.) fine buttoning needle, thread the twines through the holes previously made in the leather at the button positions so that both ends penetrate through the same hole. One twine is passed through the backing tuft of the button using the fine needle, then the two twines are knotted into the special buttoning knot, or a firmly made slip-knot (figures 10 and 11 on page 31). Ease the first four buttons down lightly, to less than maximum depth. At this stage assess whether there is sufficient filling to give a firm rounded diamond when the twines have been pulled down to their maximum depth. Should additional filling be required, it can carefully be eased in under the layers of wadding taking care to ensure that the filling remains smooth.

Whilst easing the buttons down, the flat end of a regulator should be used to fold the leather into pleats which should all lie towards the front of the seat: the creases previously hammered into the leather should assist in the folding. The depth of all the buttons should, of course, be equal. When completely set, the button twines should be tied off securely under the head of each button.

The front, back and two sides should be finished off on the underside of the seat with a bottoming tacked in position. The original chairs were finished with banding and studs around the bottom edges of the seat, but as the covering is finished on the underside this is not strictly necessary and can be omitted. As an alternative, oxidized or fancy nails may be used along the bottom edge of the seat.

The 'pin' stuffed back should be upholstered with careful support without causing too much vibration which could damage the fragile nature of the carving. Fine tacks 1 cm ($\frac{3}{8}$ in.) in length should be used throughout if possible (other than tacking off the inside back covering) to avoid too much heavy hammering. The outside back leather should be tacked on first, and the surplus trimmed off well away from the edge of the polished rebate. Two layers of skin wadding should be laid over the leather, then covered with hessian which must also be tacked away from the edge of the rebate. Webbing is unnecessary for such a small area.

If the filling of the back was removed carefully in one piece, this could be replaced in the same condition, as it would be of the correct depth and shape. A covering of calico would be beneficial prior to final covering. Before applying the covering two or three layers of wadding should be laid over the calico. The covering leather should be temporarily tacked at the bottom, stretching it to the top with further temporary tacks to remove any slackness along the length, then temporarily tacking along the two side edges.

Having cleaned out the slackness with reasonable tension all around, tack the leather home using gimp pins, then trimmed if banding and studs are to be used for finishing. If antique or fancy nails are used without banding for finishing, the gimp pins holding the leather should be temporarily tacked, only being removed progressively as the nails are hammered in position. This will avoid the gimp pins heads being visible. Plate 61 shows the chair completely restored.

62 A typical pin stuffed corner seat covered in calico ready for covering.

PIN STUFFED UPHOLSTERY

Often known as 'pin cushion' work, this is a form of flat upholstery carried out on light, delicate polished chair frames, day beds or *chaises longues*, popular on Regency period furniture and later (plate 69).

The upholstery work, which is carried out after the polishing of the frame, needs to be undertaken with considerable care, because of the fragility of the frame, closeness of the polished edge to the tacking lines, and the limited space for tacking the upholstery materials. An example of a pin-stuffed seat needing attention is shown in plate 63 with the reason for the breakdown of the seat in plate 64.

As the upholstery is carried out on the top surface of the seat frame members, a bottoming or undercovering should not be tacked on the lower surface of the seat. It will often be found that a bottom lining was omitted during the original upholstery because the webbing and hessian were set well inside the seat, and were neat enough not to need covering. Should it be desired to put on an undercovering, this should be applied and tacked folded with 1 cm ($\frac{3}{8}$ in.) tacks before the webbing is tacked into position. The traditional material for the undercovering is a black linen.

In tacking the webbing, ideally 1.2 cm ($\frac{1}{2}$ in.) fine tacks should be used, but this will depend on the condition of the wood and the width of the rebate. In many instances it will be found that the rebate is insufficiently wide for comfortable working (often a failing of the chair frame maker). If it appears too risky to use the 1.2 cm ($\frac{1}{2}$ in.) tacks, 1 cm ($\frac{3}{8}$ in.) should be used instead, and to take some of the strain off these shorter tacks, one extra strand of webbing should be put on either way in addition to the number of strands there were there originally (plate 65).

Hessian is tacked and stretched over the webbing making the fold over of the hessian and webbing one operation. Bridle ties or loops should be sewn into the hessian with the spring needle using twine, but, if a black linen undercovering has been put on before the webbing, the twine ties should not penetrate through the black linen. With deft use of the spring needle it is possible to pass the needle through the hessian: lift it slightly with the point of the needle, thus avoiding the black linen.

Generally the filling for a pin stuffed seat is horsehair as this will keep its shape, resilience and softness, but any type of filling may be used provided it is well teased and has a degree of 'life'. The filling should be applied evenly and sparingly with a very slight doming in the centre (plate 66). Then a covering of calico or lining should first be temporarily tacked to attain the shape, then tacked home, without folding the material under. The tacking line of the undercovering material should be kept well away from the polished rebated edge so that it will not show beyond the final covering.

Before applying the final covering, cotton wadding should be used as an insulation between the top and under covers to prevent the hair from working through. The sequence for applying the covering is to centre the front and back edges, temporarily tack centres front and back to ensure that the fabric is straight. After straightness is ascertained, carry on temporary tacking front and back lines towards the corners, applying a diagonal tension to the covering (as with the loose seat shown in figure 20 on page 40), then temporary tack sides. Where the sides of the seat are tapered towards the back, the covering should be tacked at the front corners first, then progressively towards the back corners. The temporary tacking stage is all important and should never be omitted. It is far easier to alter the set of covering at the temporary stage, than after it has been permanently tacked, particularly with this form of work. The covering should now be tacked home without being folded under, using 1 cm ($\frac{3}{8}$ in.) fine tacks: the tacked edges should be

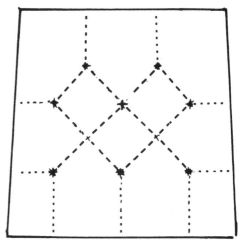

75 *Leather marked and creased for seat.*

63 An example of a 'pin' stuffed or 'pin' cushion seat needing re-upholstery.

64 Webbing broken away from the rebate on a pin stuffed seat.

65 Replacing of webbing on pin stuffed seat.

66 Tucking horse hair under bridle ties in pin stuffed seat.

kept as flat as possible to allow the gimp to lie flat. Keep the tacks clear of the polished edge so that the covering may be trimmed away with a sharp bladed knife, also clear of the polished edge. The gimp or braid should be fixed in position by starting at a back corner and using an adhesive such as Seccotine or Copydex, applied with a spatula or brush. Temporary gimp pins or small tacks can be used to hold the gimp or braid in place.

Pin stuffed backs on small chairs may need the outside back applied first as with a black linen undercovering similar to that of the seat, described on page 109. The back should then be upholstered in the same way as the seat was. On other types of pin stuffed backs the outside back may be applied to the outer side of the frame, in which case a gimp is needed for both the inside and outside.

67 Chaise longue frame with upholstery stripped.

Larger pin stuffed items, such as day beds or *chaises longues* (plates 67 to 69), are upholstered in a similar way to the small seat but on a larger scale. Often the larger seats carry a deep squab cushion as shown in plate 19 on page 30. Seat webbing should be applied generously in these cases.

68 Seat 'pin' stuffed with base hessian on back to support back filling.

69 Completed chaise longue with squab cushion.

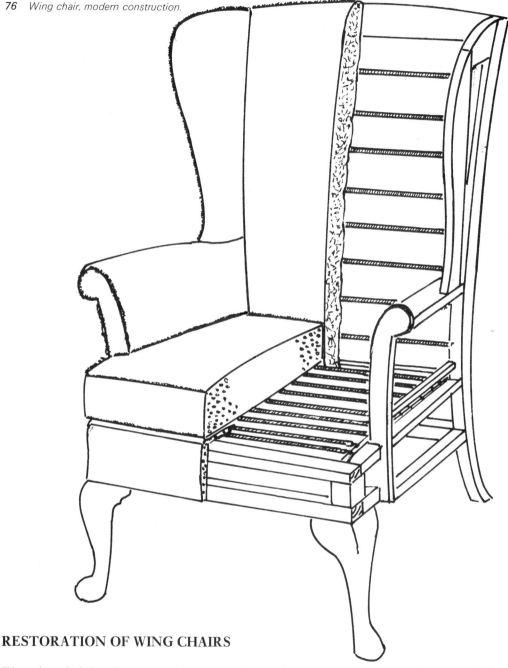

RESTORATION OF WING CHAIRS

The wing chair has been a popular style of chair since the Queen Anne period, when it was developed. The chair's side 'flaps' shield the sitter from draughts and also, should he fall asleep, prevent his head from slipping off the back of the chair. There are many different styles and designs of wing chairs; some are covered in soft fabric, some in leather, the latter often being deeply buttoned. These are particularly attractive, but need skill in their restoration. Figures 76 and 77 show different constructions of wing chairs.

77 *Wing chair, traditional construction.*

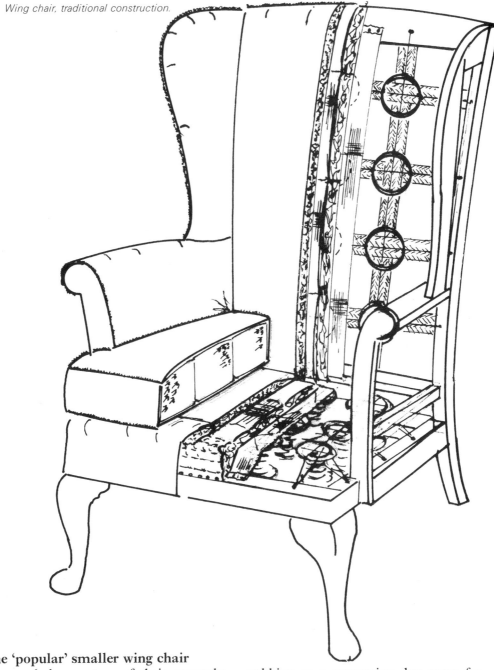

The 'popular' smaller wing chair

Figure 76 shows a type of chair currently produced for the popular market. The majority of those sold in recent years are rather smaller in size than the earlier models, and are upholstered with modern pre-formed materials by modern production methods. Sometimes these have rubber webbing as a suspension, but more frequently they have tension spring suspension for the seats (figure 49 on page 70), and a lighter gauge spring for the back, with two or three strands of heavier gauge at the base to give firmer support to the lumbar region (plates 70 and 71).

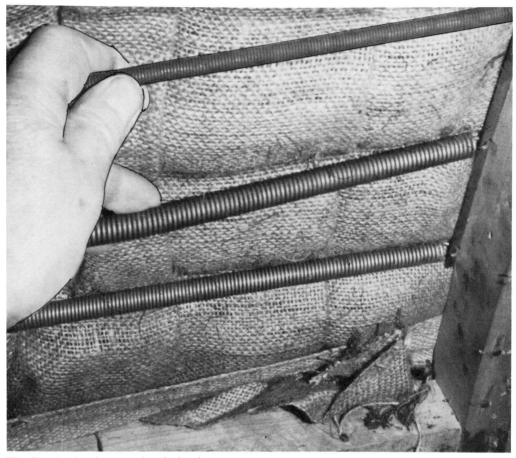

70 Showing heavier gauge 'tension' springs at base of back to give firmer support to lumbar region.

The arms may have foam or rubberized hair filling, or hair padding needled on to hessian with an overlay of cotton felt. Filling for the back may be loose kapok contained in a cotton case stitched through to hold the kapok in position, the case being tacked in position on the back frame rails, or a layer of foam may be laid over the springing with hessian as an insulation between. The thinly stuffed wings may contain a layer of hair and wadding or thin foam encased in cotton felt, or possibly one or two layers of cotton felt only. Quite often the wings will need no attention other than recovering. The cushions would be filled with latex or polyurethane foam.

Re-upholstery of this type of chair is simpler than of the chair using traditional loose fillings or materials. On examination it may be found that the seat tension springs have become over-stretched and damaged (plate 48 on page 71). The damaged springs should be replaced. These can easily be un-hooked, as shown in plate 49 on page 72, and the new springs hooked on to the side plates in their places. The correct size of springs must be used for replacement, otherwise they will give a different deflection from the original with resulting unevenness. The springs should be approximately eight per cent shorter (including the end hooks) than the distance between the

71 Hessian must be tacked with an amount of slackness over a tension-sprung back.

fixing plates, for example, if the distance between the plates is 45.5 cm (18 in.), the length of the spring should be 42 cm (16½ in.).

If, as there probably will be, difficulty in obtaining replacement springs, the simplest and easiest method of restoring such a seat is to replace the tension springs with rubber webbing. This, in fact, will give a far more satisfactory suspension for the cushion than the original tension springs. To do this *all* the tension springs must be removed. Do not replace only the damaged springs with rubber webbing. The metal plates must be unscrewed, and the inner top edges of the seat rails must have the sharp edges re-

moved with a wood rasp to prevent chaffing or abrasion of the webbing (plate 50 on page 73). Rubber webbing 5 cm (2 in.) wide should be used to replace the springs, five or six strands being tacked from side to side. The tension of each strand should be the same: mark the webbing for tensioning as explained in an earlier chapter, and see that a tension of approximately eight to ten per cent is given to the webbing.

The covering for the front lip of the seat should be attached as shown in plate 72. One edge of the covering (or a fly piece) is tacked on the top surface of the front rail. The covering is then taken *under* the first web and brought *over* the top of the web.

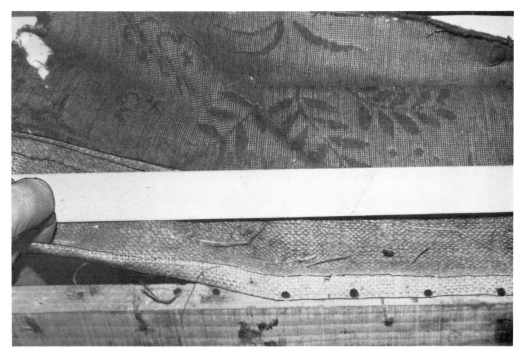

A thin filling is inserted under the cover, which is brought over the front of the seat, and tacked on the underside of the rail. Plate 73 shows the front cover tacked in position, and also a strip of covering hemmed on the inside line, joined by mitring to the front piece, and tacked under the side rail to hide the tacked ends of the rubber webbing.

In the majority of cases, the arms will need some extra padding to give them more resilience. A piece of 2.5 cm (1 in.) foam cut to size may be used for this. It is held in place by strips of calico or similar fabric stuck around the edges and tacked into position to form the contours of the arm. The arm covering may be put immediately over the foam if desired without any wadding or felt between. The original tack holes will give an indication of where the outside arm covering will hide the tacks used to hold the inside arm covering. The back should be re-covered after the arm covering has been tacked into position, followed by the inside wing covering.

Cutting the covering round the stiles (frame members which impede the covering from being laid smoothly) should be done carefully so as not to leave the cut in the cover visible, or allow the covering to be slack so that it pulls away from the stile showing the interior filling. There are many instances in upholstery covering where there are difficult cuts around stiles: see page 32. As a reinforcement for the covering the outside wings, outside arms and outside back should be lined with hessian after covering the inside back.

A piping or ruche may be tacked in one length round the edge of the wings and across the back. Outside arms should be back-tacked (figure 5 on page 24), along the rail on the underside of the roll of the arm, and tacked on the underside of the base rail and the outside line of the back leg. They should be pinned temporarily, and then slip-stitched to the side of the front facing. If the top line of the outside back is straight, that also may be back-tacked, then brought down, and the bottom edge of the covering

72 Method of attaching covering to front of chair taking it under front strand of rubber webbing.

73 Front of seat covered with a strip of covering tacked along the side members to cover the tacked ends of the rubber webbing.

tacked on the underside of the base rail. The long sides of the outside back should be first pinned, as were the outside arms, and then slip-stitched along the whole length from top to bottom. An undercovering or bottoming should be tacked into position to cover the raw edges of the fabric and to give a presentable appearance.

The foam cushion will in most cases need replacing. Over a number of years its resistance to loading deteriorates, resulting in a loss in depth and thickness. The cushion interior will not hold the sitter up from the base suspension. If the interior is replaced with latex foam it is wise to fit an under-covering of closely woven calico or linen before fitting the final covering, since latex, whilst superior to urethane, will rapidly deteriorate if exposed to strong sunlight, even if it is filtered through a woven covering. An undercovering will greatly reduce the surface powdering which strong sunlight causes. Urethane foam is not affected in this way. Foam 7.5 cm or 10 cm (3 in. or 4 in.) deep is suitable for cushioning, the

deeper one, of course, giving more comfort. A foam of suitable density must be used for cushioning. Some of the urethane foams are ultra-soft: they are not intended for cushioning, and, therefore, should not be used for this purpose.

One of the arts of applying upholstery covering is knowing how to tension the fabric to remove the fullness and to get the required contours. Figure 78 shows various parts of a chair and suitable tension points.

The larger wing chair

Restoration of the larger and more elaborate wing chair (plate 74) with a traditional construction will pose rather more problems than the wing chairs mentioned so far. Many of the more expensive chairs will have a double cone deeply sprung seat with a spring edge (figure 41 on page 66). If the main springs in the well of the seat have become displaced or buckled and need replacement invariably the edge springs will also need attention. It is unwise to replace one without replacing the other.

74 Traditional wing chair covered in leather.

4 Victorian nursing chair
restored and covered in red velvet

5 Tub easy chair and
foot stool re-upholstered
and covered in velvet

6 Reproduction Chippendale armchair
buttoned in leather

Do not attempt to re-use any materials such as the webbing, hessian and scrim once they have been removed. Whilst they may appear sound, after a period of years the fibres in the yarn and the weave deteriorate and once disturbed their life is comparatively short. If these materials are re-used, a further repair will become necessary in a short time.

Once all the old seat materials have been removed, webbing supporting the seat springs should be tacked in position using 1.6 cm ($\frac{5}{8}$ in.) tacks (figure 39). The majority of average size seats have nine springs in the well with four on the edge if it is a sprung edge. Plate 75 shows a seat with a firm front edge without any springs, these being replaced by a rail fixed between the arms to which the spring hessian is tacked. If desired, a sprung edge may be replaced with a rail across the front of the seat ensuring, of course, that it is securely fixed into the side of each arm member. Figure 41 on page 66 shows the positioning of the springs in the seat. How the lashing is

done is explained in an earlier chapter (figures 40 and 41 on pages 64 and 66).

When positioning the hessian over the springs, a gutter must be formed as shown in figure 46 on page 69. The tension of the hessian over the springs should be just sufficient to remove the slackness but not so tight as to reduce the height of the springs. First tack the hessian without folding it over using 1.6 cm ($\frac{5}{8}$ in.) improved tacks. Trim off the surplus leaving enough to fold over, and add a further line of tacks for reinforcement, as a great deal of stress is placed upon the spring hessian. The hessian over the spring edge should be left temporarily tacked in position until the front edge stitching of the scrim is completed. The top coils of the springs are then sewn through the hessian (plate 45 on page 65), using a curved spring needle similar to that used on the base webbing. Three or four ties may be used.

75 Chair seat without spring edge. Showing rail across front of seat dowelled into arms with supporting block in centre.

78   Tension points for covering.

Rows of bridle ties should now be sewn into the hessian; they should be sufficiently slack to enable the fibre filling to be tucked into them. Infilling with the fibre should start round the sides and back with a fairly firm density to withstand the tension of the covering at these places. The centre can then be infilled as required.

With the first stuffing in position, scrim should be laid over the filling, tucked down through the spaces under the arm and back stay rails, and temporarily tacked with the larger tacks along the top edge of the base seat rail only. As a temporary fixing for the scrim on the front edge cane, skewers should be used as shown in plate 76.

Whilst the scrim is held in position in this manner, twine ties (plate 77) should be run through the scrim and filling with a long needle. Start the first tie at a back corner approximately 7.5 to 10 cm (3 to 4 in.) in from the sides and back lines of the seat. Push the needle through the scrim from the top surface of the seat so that the eye of the needle and twine go through last. Draw the point of the needle through the base of the seat and through the webbing or spacing between the webbing (depending on how the webbing is positioned). Do not draw the needle and twine all the way through the seat: the twine should pass only through the hessian covering the springs. Having felt the twine pass through the hessian, hold the pointed end of the needle and direct it so that it passes back through the hessian approximately 1.2 cm ($\frac{1}{2}$ in.) away from its entry point. Make a slip-knot to prevent the twine being pulled out. Carry the twine across the surface of the scrim for 15 to 20 cm (6 to 8 in.), and make another entry into the scrim and filling carrying out the same procedure as previously described but without the slip-knot. From beginning to end of this stage the twine should be a running line, knotted only at its start and finish. The last tie should initially have only a temporary knot. The ties should be tightened after all are inserted. Start with the second loop through the scrim between the ties, hold the twine in the fingers of the left hand, run the fingers of the right hand along the twine to compress the filling and scrim, and at the same time pull the twine tight with the other hand, so that the ties make indentations in the filling. The purpose of this operation is to ensure that the filling is locked in position and unable to shift. An easy chair seat will need three to four ties each side and back and front (including the corner ties). With settees the ties are continued across in approximately the same sequence. It is advisable to temporarily knot the last tie only so that the depth of the indentation of the ties may be adjusted if necessary after the front edge has been stitched.

A seat intended to carry a cushion should have a thinner filling over shorter springs than a full seat which does not have a cushion. The cushion seat should appear flat. In fact, the front edge of the lip should be slightly higher than the centre area of the seat so that the cushion will lie flat on its

76 Skewers holding scrim in position temporarily
on to line of cane.

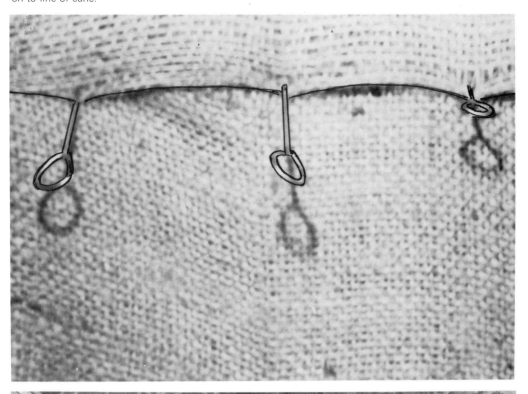

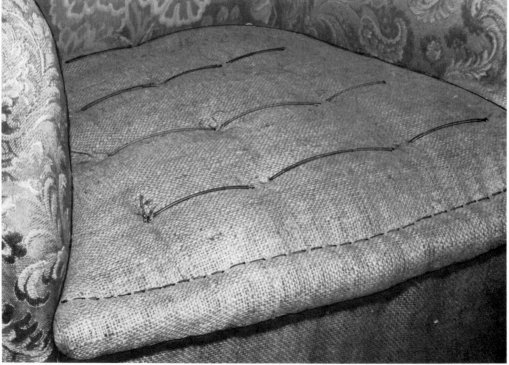

77 Easy chair seat 'first' stuffed showing stuffing
ties and stitched 'under the edge' roll on front.
This is a 'full' seat, not needing a cushion.

platform without a gap being visible under the front edge between the lip and the base of the cushion (plates 78 and 79).

Once the tying in process is completed, the skewers holding the scrim on to the front cane can be taken out, and the filling re-arranged more uniformly. It is difficult to arrange this perfectly in the first instance. The skewers should then be replaced rather more closely together this time, to hold the folded-under scrim more evenly than before. The scrim should now be sewn with a cir-cular needle threaded with twine to the hessian along the line of the cane: a blanket or oversewing stitch may be used. The yarn of the scrim should run parallel with the front of the seat. The scrim or hessian is much more difficult to work and a good roll impossible to achieve if the fabric weave is out of straight. Plate 77 above shows an under the edge front with a stitched roll. After the scrim has been sewn to the hessian at the cane edge, blind stitch (figures 31 to 34 on page 56) immediately above the line of cane (not any distance from it). This will make for a firm roll by drawing the filling towards it. The roll stitch must be made along the same line as the blind-stitch and *not* spaced away from it. As the roll stitch is being formed the twine should be tightened so that it gives a good indentation: it is made as the top stitch in figure 36 on page 58, but taking in more filling and scrim.

Having completed the roll stitch, tack the scrim home on the top surface of the rails using large improved tacks along the side and back members of the seat. The hessian of the spring edge can now be tacked per-manently using 1.6 cm ($\frac{5}{8}$ in.) improved tacks. A rule should be used to ensure that the cane or wire edge is level with the base along its complete length, particularly in the case of a settee. It is wise to leave the tacking home of the hessian until this stage because the end springs often reduce slightly in height during stitching and give an uneven line. This can be rectified at this

point if necessary.

After inserting bridle ties in appropriate positions distribute the second stuffing (normally hair) over the surface of the scrim. A seat of this type is better with an under-covering of calico or similar cheap material. The undercovering should be approximately the same size of the covering with flys. It should be laid immediately over the filling without wadding. The wadding should be applied *over* the undercovering under the top covering. Even at this stage temporary tacking of the undercovering is necessary. It should be tucked through the sides and back under the stay rails, and tacked on the top surface of the base rails. As with the scrim, fix the front of the material to the spring edge with skewers, cleaning out the fullness, and tensioning before stitching under the edge with a circular needle and thread. The seat should be 'sat out' or tested before finally tacking home the undercovering.

The final covering should be put on the seat in the same manner as the under-covering, not forgetting the wadding to prevent the hair (if being used) from work-ing through the covering. Hessian flys should be used to economize on covering fabric.

Plate 80 shows a wing chair in the process of restoration. The seat and back had deteriorated so much that they needed to be completely stripped out, but the first stuffing of the arms and wings was satisfactory enough to be left in position and re-used with a new second stuffing plus an under-covering of calico. This situation is common as the arms and wings do not have to with-stand so much tension on the fillings, hes-sian and scrim.

78   Stuffed back of tub easy chair. Springs sewn in seat and lashed with edge spring in position. Constructed for cushion seat.

79   Construction of a cushion seat. The 'lip' formed as front of seat with spring edge.

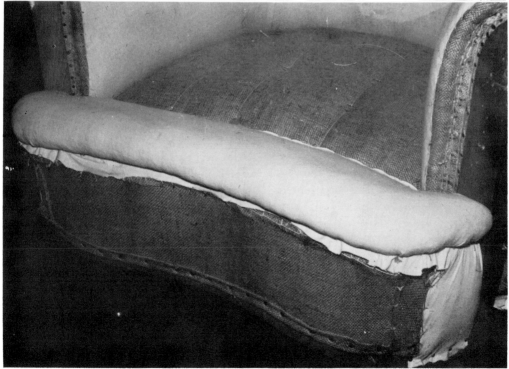

In this particular example, there are additional rails along the sides of the seat and across the back to which the seat spring hessian and scrim must be tacked. This type of frame construction reinforces the sides and back of the seat and keeps them from dropping too low with the tension of the covering, thus preventing a possible gap between the base of the arm and top of the seat.

After the seat has been covered, the arms and wings should be top stuffed. Calico is used as an undercovering over the original first stuffing. Sometimes it is necessary to run another stitching line around the front roll of arms and wings as a reinforcement if the rolls feel a little slack. Bridle ties are necessary in the arms as in other parts of the upholstery to hold the top filling in place. The covering around the front roll is tightly tensioned from the base of the arm to the outside point of the scroll to reduce the amount of pleating needed around the radius of the scroll. The covering is pinned out under the edge, and then sewn using a circular needle and thread. The facing is cut to shape, piped and sewn under the edge.

It will be noted that the strands of webbing on the back are positioned in such a way as to support twelve springs, 12.5 cm (5 in.) in height. The bottom row of springs being of 11 S.W.G., are a gauge heavier than those above, which are 12 S.W.G. To prevent the back springs from sagging downward with the weight of the filling they should be tilted slightly at an upward angle and lashed, preferably through the centres only, using a length of double twine. This method of lashing is more suitable for the lighter gauge springs of a back, whereas the heavier laidcord is used for lashing the seat.

The hessian covering the springs is put on with a slightly slack tension, and the tops of the springs are sewn to it, in the same way as the seat springs were sewn to the hessian of the seat. When inserting the first stuffing

under the bridle ties, it should be lighter in density than that put into the seat to retain the softness of the lighter gauge springs. The scrim over the back filling should also be laid on loosely. On no account should it be tensioned tightly as this will force the filling flat, and make the back firmer than it need be. Ample ties should be run through the scrim and filling of the back to keep the filling in position. The tapered back of the wing chair shown in plate 80, has the effect of reducing the thickness at the top back rail and requires a minimum thickness of filling directly on the rail. A row of stitching may be needed along the top rail, but this will depend upon the original style of the back. It is desirable to put an undercovering over the second stuffing, before applying two or three layers of wadding and, finally, the top covering.

Most wing chairs have three stiles round which the cover has to be cut on each side of the back. These are hidden from view when the filling and covering are in position. By forcing one's fingers between the chair back and the wings and arms, the stiles can, however, be felt, and their position should be noted before the back is installed. The method of cutting the covering round the stiles is shown in figure 14 on page 33. Before attempting the cutting, it is most important to ensure that the fabric is lying on the back square with the framework. If the cuts are made with the material out of square, they will not allow the fabric to pull tightly round the stiles. Consequently the cuts will gape, and show the filling below. Where the inside arm has a fairly large curve projecting into the back line, a collar should be fitted as shown in figure 13 on page 32. This is particularly important if the covering is leather.

The facings are applied before the outside arms are covered. The facing covering is cut a little larger than its finished size. It is then pinned out under the edge and the outside is tacked on the outside edge of the facing frame member. If soft fabric is being used, the join under the edge may be finished with piping or upholstery cord sewn along the join line of the arm and facing.

The outside arms, back, and wings should be interlined with hessian as reinforcement. The outside wings should be pinned out around the outer line, and then slip-stitched. The lower line is tacked along the underside of the arm rail; the outside arm is then back-tacked (figure 5 on page 24), along the top line under the roll of the arm with the lower edge of the covering tacked on the underside of the base rail. The outside back may be back-tacked if the top rail is straight, but for curved or shaped top rails back-tacking is inappropriate: the fabric must be pinned out temporarily, then slip-stitched. The underside is usually finished off with bottoming, and the base line often covered with fringe or braid.

80 Restoration of wing easy chair, first stuffing of arms and wings being retained.

79 *The first stuffed scroll arm. Large roll stitched on outer top edges.*

VARIATIONS IN UPHOLSTERED ARMS AND BACKS

A wide variety of arm styles and methods of upholstery were used in the earlier traditional work. The upholstery and covering of an arm is probably the most difficult part of restoring an easy chair or settee.

The scroll arm

Each different stage of development of the upholstered chair produced its own particular style of arms. Of these, the scroll arm is the most difficult shape to restore owing to its contours and sculptured appearance. Since even experienced upholsterers often have some difficulty in producing a true pair of arms, the learner must also expect to have this problem.

As already mentioned in dealing with the restoration of wing chairs, the first stuffing of a scroll arm (or any other style of traditionally upholstered arm) may well be in sufficiently good condition to leave in position, so that only the second stuffing and covering need attention. Where the condition and stability of the arm materials are suspect, it is advisable to re-upholster the arm completely while the rest of the chair or settee is being restored. This will prevent the arms deteriorating at a later stage whilst the rest of the work is in good condition.

Figures 79 to 82 show a variety of arm styles which may well be encountered in the restoration of an old piece of upholstery. The scroll arm shown on the wing chair in figure 76 on page 114 shows a firmly stuffed arm, that is, with the inside arm lined with hessian which is stretched tightly between the arm stay rail and the top arm rail to make a base for the filling. The filling is then arranged on the hessian to give the required thickness to the inside arm (this generally should be of minimum thickness to give ample width of seat between the arms). The scroll, or top part, of the arm is then filled with sufficient stuffing to form the shape through to the back of the arm. This stuffing may be rubberized hair, or fibre padding and felt, or some other preformed type of filling.

81 Fixing of springs on to arm rail.

An alternative to the firmly stuffed scroll is the sprung scroll arm. This gives a larger radius to the scroll shape and a more resilient roll along the top of the arm. Plate 81 shows the method of fixing springs to the top rail of an arm, usually four, sometimes five, springs will suffice along the length of the arm rail.

A light gauge (12 S.W.G.) spring should be used to give the correct degree of softness. Unfortunately sprung arms are often damaged by being sat on. The upholstery of the arm is not intended to take the full weight of a person, and consequently the light gauge springs become distorted and incapable of pushing the filling back into its original shape. The remedy for this is to use a heavier gauge spring (say, 11 S.W.G.) which will withstand rougher treatment but not give such satisfactory softness.

The springs should be spaced evenly along the arm rail, and held in position with wire staples 1.2 cm ($\frac{1}{2}$ in.) in length. Alternatively, they can be fixed by means of a length of webbing first tacked at each end; the base coils of the springs are then slipped under the webbing, and improved tacks are hammered home on each side of the spring wire in four positions (plate 81, above). To prevent 'chattering' (the lower coils tapping the tacks), a double strip of hessian or waste fabric of double thickness should be laid over the base coils in one length from front to back with two tacks between the springs to hold the insulating piece in position.

Once the springs are positioned and fixed along each of the arm rails, they should be eased down slightly and lashed to prevent any lateral movement, and to hold them under tension (figure 80). Two strands of webbing should then be stretched (by hand only) over the surface of the top coils from the front to the back of the arm, and tacked to the top edge of the front timber scroll and to the back frame with large improved tacks. The webbing should be tacked so that it makes a flat platform along the length of the arm over the springs. The top coils should then be sewn to the webbing again to prevent any lateral movement.

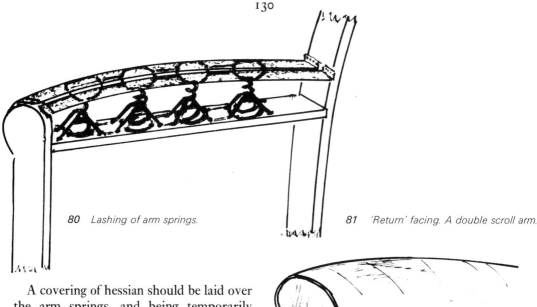

80 *Lashing of arm springs.*

81 *'Return' facing. A double scroll arm.*

A covering of hessian should be laid over the arm springs, and being temporarily tacked into position. It is most important that the weave of the hessian lies straight and parallel with the webs. In some instances, a pleat on the front and back corners will be unavoidable in the hessian. After removing as much looseness from the hessian as possible it may be tacked home. The height of the springs should be such that there is a slight rise from the front of the arm to the first spring and a slight drop from the last spring to the tacking position on the back frame. Again, the hessian should be sewn to the top coils of the springs, just as the seat springs were sewn to the seat hessian. This completes the springing stage for the arm.

The stuffing of the arm should now be proceeded with as previously described, with ample bridle ties inserted. The filling should be fairly light. If it is too dense, it will prevent the light gauge springs from returning to their full height after being compressed. Scrim should be temporarily tacked over the first stuffing with the weave running straight along the top of the scroll, from front to back: the shaping of the arm will cause the weave to drop down to the back corner. When the scrim is temporarily tacked, stuffing ties should be run through the inside arm to prevent the filling from

dropping. Figure 79 shows the ties and the tacking of the scrim around the front scroll. The front scroll needs a blind-stitch and a roll stitch to give the under-the-edge effect if a facing is being piped or corded to hide the join. A fairly large roll should be stitched on the outside line of the arm from front to back. An undercovering of calico is advisable before the top covering on the arm; a better shape will be obtained through this extra effort.

The double scroll facing, often referred to as return facing (figure 81), has an additional scroll to the base of the arm. The particular difficulty in this lies in arranging the fullness around the two scrolls when tacking the scrim. It is advisable not to have too much filling around the facing; allow only sufficient for as thin a roll as possible.

82 'Capped on' arm. Piping on each edge.

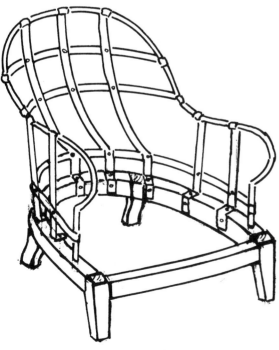

84 The Victorian iron back.

The pad and panel arm

The pad and panel arm (figure 83), is a relatively simple arm to upholster. The pad on the top of the arm rail is upholstered with a roll on each side of the wide arm rail, the gap between being filled with hair, and covered first with calico or other under-covering. The space between the arm rail and stay rail at the bottom of the arm is lined with hessian: this is best done before the pad is applied to the top rail. The inside arm panels may be back-tacked along the line below the pad or the covering may be tacked normally with the tack line covered by braid, gimp or fringe.

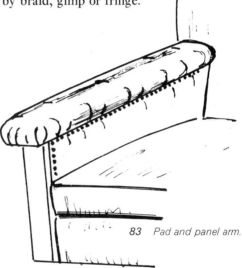

83 Pad and panel arm.

The iron back

A popular method of constructing the back (and sometimes arm) framework of many Victorian chairs, etc., was with 1.6 cm ($\frac{5}{8}$ in.) iron rod and steel laths, fabricated to the contours of the back (figure 84). This type of construction will often be met with when restoring Victorian upholstery. The iron rods were shaped around formers so each came out alike. The top ends of the metal laths were riveted or welded to the rod, and their lower ends were screwed to the timber base seat frame.

The iron back was considered to have two advantages over a timber construction:

one was its springiness or lack of rigidity as compared with its timber counterpart; the other was its cheapness: the iron back with its compound curves was more easily made by the metal worker without the wastage involved in cutting shapes from timber.

As all of the frame, apart from the seat, was metal, the upholstery materials could not be tacked to the back and arms, but had to be hand stitched with a circular needle and twine. This took rather longer than the conventional method of tacking. Many upholsterers considered this was too time consuming, and too 'fiddly', so eventually the iron back disappeared, because practical upholsterers were becoming conscious of mass production methods. However, at a later date, circumstances forced many upholstery manufacturers to produce a wide range of iron and steel upholstery frames. This situation occurred shortly after the second world war, when the Board of Trade wartime restrictions on furniture manufacture were eased. At that time suitable timber for upholstery frames was still scarce and also very expensive. Many manufacturers were, therefore, compelled to return to metal once again.

Easy chairs and settees were constructed with metal frames of different types. Some were made from flat pressed steel, fabricated by machinery which had earlier been used for the war effort. These frames had narrow compressed papier mâché fillets fixed to them in what were intended to be appropriate positions for tacking purposes, but the upholsterer found it difficult to produce a sufficiently tensioned final covering as the paper fillets were often in the wrong positions, or they would not hold the tacks. The customer was often dissatisfied so that type of metal frame soon disappeared from the scene, although there is the odd occasion when one will turn up for re-upholstery.

Angle iron frames were also introduced at about the same time, since iron and steel were more readily obtainable than timber.

These frames were, however, extremely heavy, and they, too, had fixing problems, which were overcome to some extent by fixing timber rails in positions for tacking. These frames, too, soon disappeared from the upholstery workshops as timber became more freely available.

The firm of Ernest Race was probably the most successful manufacturer of metal frame upholstery, and also one of the first manufacturers to use urethane foam successfully. One particular model, known as the Race chair, became extremely popular, and sold in thousands. This chair had a modern design, even by today's standards, and incorporated a very clever upholstery technique. It was, however, still all sewn by hand.

Normally the iron back wears well, as very little can go wrong with the frame, and the basic upholstery is often in good condition. It is wise, however, to test the base hessian and webbing for soundness, particularly if the back has been buttoned, or buttoning is planned. If either of these has deteriorated it must be replaced with new materials, as a good deal of sewing takes place on the hessian, and also the button twines may pull through it.

When the old hessian has been removed, ensure that the steel rod around the outside line and the laths are encased with strips of hessian or other material (plate 82). This should be wrapped tightly round them so that it will not twist, then the ends are sewn tightly. This prevents any rusting of the metal which would cause roughness which, in turn, would soon wear through the hessian supporting the filling as this is compressed and released during use. It is also an aid in sewing the materials to the frame. The replacement hessian should be cut roughly to shape, then skewered into position, folded under, and wrapped around the steel rods. Then oversew with a circular needle and twine, so that the whole area inside the iron shape has a firm support for the filling. The threads of the hessian should be laid perfectly straight up and down and across.

To give depth to the back, a roll is made around the back edge (plate 83), so that there is an under-the-edge effect on the outside line of the back. The roll should be formed by sewing a strip of scrim or lightweight hessian approximately 20 to 25 cm (8 to 10 in.) wide to the inside back hessian some 10 cm (4 in.) in from the edge of the back, drawing a chalk line for a guide, then temporarily skewering the roll material into position. Where the roll is to negotiate the curve of the back, an amount of fullness should be worked into the scrim or hessian used for the roll where it is being sewn on to the inside back hessian. This is because the outside line of the roll will need far more material than the inside line where it is sewn. The roll should be well filled and firmly stitched to prevent any looseness or movement when the covering has been

fixed in position. Having the roll in position, the arms should be stuffed (these are usually much smaller than an arm on a conventional timber frame), covered in scrim and stitched again. As there is no timber to tack to, the scrim must be sewn to the hessian, or the material wrapped round the metal frame.

The back and arms are normally worked separately. The arms are covered first with the back covering being pleated at the join between the two, with a button holding the pleat or fold in position. Before filling in the back with stuffing, positions for the buttons should be marked with tailor's chalk on the inside back hessian. The original hessian, if it has been retained, will give an indication of how the buttons were previously positioned. The marking should be taken from

82 Iron back chair showing hessian covering and hessian strips round the laths.

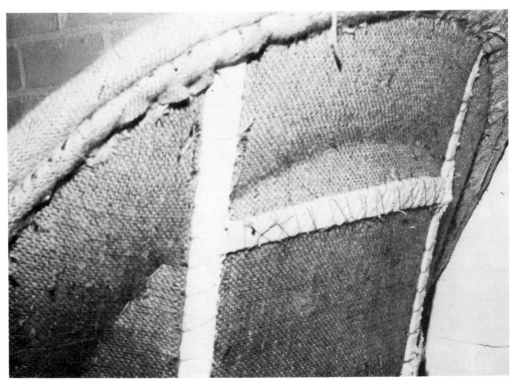

this, and the button ties should be fixed in as previously described on page 105. The buttoning should then be carried out in a similar way. If a fabric is used instead of leather, it is not necessary to pierce the covering beforehand at the button positions, or to crease the covering. It is important to

remember not to pull the buttons down to the maximum depth in the first instance. This should be done only when all the buttons have been successfully arranged with the pleating forming the diamonds between the buttons nicely arranged. Butterflies (small strips of hessian) should be inserted under the twine loops to prevent the twine from pulling through the hessian.

83 Iron back chair showing roll round back edge.

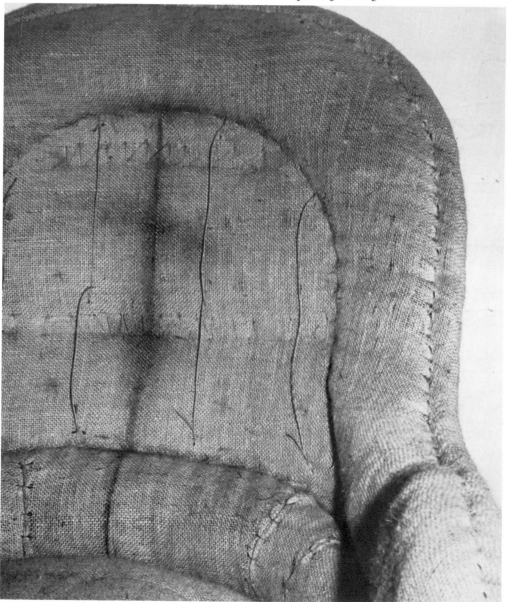

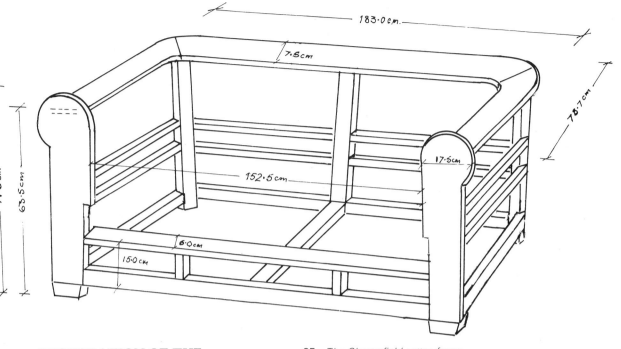

RESTORATION OF THE CHESTERFIELD

85   The Chesterfield settee frame.

Restoration of the ever-popular Victorian Chesterfield settee, named after an Earl of Chesterfield, is a major undertaking, even for the professional upholsterer. Previous experience of upholstery work is essential, particularly if the piece is to be re-covered in leather.

While Chesterfields are usually settees, Chesterfield suites (a settee with two matching easy chairs) were often produced in earlier days. The chairs themselves are virtually small settees with almost as much work involved in their upholstery as the settee itself. Versions of the Chesterfield settee currently produced for the popular market look somewhat like the originals, but are now upholstered by a method quite different from the traditional one. Pre-formed springing and fillings are used with a consequent saving in production time. Even so, covering a Chesterfield, particularly in leather, is still hard work for the upholsterer involving many changes in

working position for the craftsman, and additionally the Chesterfield is heavy to move about.

Restoration and re-covering of a traditionally upholstered Chesterfield invariably involves complete reseating. In the majority of cases, the webbing will have broken and sagging strands will be resting on the floor, owing to the shallow 'bun' or short square feet usually found on these items. Because the webbing has collapsed, the springing has usually become crippled, and needs replacing. A further fault frequently found is that the cane of the spring edge will have been broken in one or two places which, in turn, may have allowed the edge springs to buckle.

The upholstery of the seat should be thoroughly examined: to apply covering to a faulty seat is a complete waste of effort and money. The top line of springs on the back of the settee should also be examined. Unfortunately, the back of a Chesterfield is a convenient height for sitting on. The springs used in the back are of a light gauge, and are easily damaged in this way. However, in most cases, the first stuffing of the back and arms is satisfactory, so only the second stuffing needs attention. As with all buttoned work which is being re-covered, the original covering should be carefully stripped off and used as a guide and template for the marking of the new covering. The diamond shapes, which may have become formed in the material over the years, must be flattened first.

Figure 85 shows a Chesterfield settee frame. There may be slight variations in construction, size, and sections of timber. It will be noted that the illustration shows the front edge springs will be sited along a rail built up from the base rail. This allows shorter springs to be used making the edge more stable. But examples will be found of tall springs set upon the base rail. Where this occurs, it is advisable to adapt the edge as shown in the illustration, since taller springs tend to buckle if not correctly lashed.

In a large number of instances it will be found that the seat webbing has been applied to the top surface of the base seat stretchers (rails). The Chesterfield seat is normally very deeply sprung; even with webbing on the top of these rails a fairly tall spring is required, perhaps 30 to 40 cm (10 to 12 in.). If webbed on the base even taller springs would be required.

Before applying webbing to the top surface of the seat rails, the inner corners of the rails should be rasped to remove the sharp edge which would cause wear to the webbing. A further safeguard to prolong the life of the webbing is to tack a strip of webbing, hessian, or some other material to the top and inside of the rails so that it will prevent the webbing from bearing down directly on to the corner of the rail. This precaution will add many years to the life of the webbing. Ample webs should be used,

and taken *over* the cross members or iron bracing bars. Where webbing is tacked on the underside of the frame, it should also be under the cross members. Additional support should be given by tacking a length of webbing along the cross member over the long strands going from side to side. The short strand of web running along the cross member should be tacked *only between* the long strands (figure 86), and not through the long strands side to side. This is to enable the stretch of the web to equalize itself between the cross members as it slips through the supporting length.

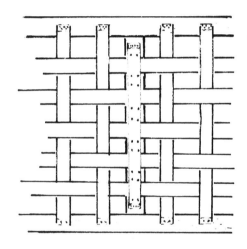

86   Support of webbing.

As indicated earlier, the tall springs in the seat must be double lashed, that is, across the top coils first, as with normal lashing, then through the centre of the spring to avoid any lateral movement of the centre coils. It is essential to lash the top coils first to attain the correct height. If the centres are done first, the top lashing will slightly reduce the height and thus the centre lashing will slacken. It is advisable, in the first instance, to lash springs across the shortest distance, and then follow with the longer lengths. Figure 87 shows a cut through section of a Chesterfield settee.

87 *Section through Chesterfield settee.*

Seat springs are covered with good quality hessian, and stuffed and stitched in the usual way, with an under-the-edge roll rather heavier than is normally required for an easy chair seat. A plainly covered seat will need additional strips along each side selvedge as the normal fabric would not be sufficiently wide. The width of the additional strips depends upon the seat width of the settee. Flys may be used on the sides of the seat covering and along the back line to economize in the use of covering material. If the seat is to be deeply buttoned, the lines of buttons and width of diamonds should match those of the back. Vandyking of the covering will be necessary (figures 68 to 71 on page 99). This will enable the joins to be hidden under the pleating between the buttoning.

If leather is used, a critical part of covering the seat is the fitting, cutting and welting of the leather under the roll edge. To attempt this successfully, care and patience is required. If a buttonless seat is being worked, the leather may be tem-porarily tacked in position, pinned along the cane under the edge, and trimmed off leaving sufficient for seaming. The top front border should be cut with a straight edge along its total length, except the final 10 cm (4 in.) each end which should be trimmed off the straight, removing about 1.2 cm ($\frac{1}{2}$ in.). This will eradicate wrinkling along the ends of the border when finished. The border should be positioned and notched together with the seat, so that when sewn it will be in its true position. The pleats at the front corners of the seat should be arranged and marked on the border as a guide to correct positioning. When sewn together the welted join should be skewered into position along the cane under the edge, then sewn with strong linen thread to the hessian using a circular needle. This operation will ensure that the welting will remain in position throughout the life of the leather. As there are normally two borders on the front, the bottom border may be back-tacked. This should be slightly wider than the upper border.

Plates 84 and 85 show the first stuffing of a Chesterfield easy chair back and arm, and the one arm of a settee. The ground-work marking is shown for the deep buttoning. It will be noted that a hole has been made in the scrim at one button position (plate 85), the scrim being snipped with the point of the scissors, then the hole enlarged by pushing a finger through to make a bed for the button to sink into. This should be repeated at each button position. The covering of the back and arms are best done separately. Plate 86 shows an arm in the process of being covered. The join between the back and the arm is hidden under the pleating and held in position with the buttons through the leather. Plate 87 shows arms and back covered.

Where the Chesterfield design is being upholstered from the virgin frame, it is more convenient to work on the back and arms before doing any work to the seat. This enables work to be done on the back from all angles, including through the seat frame. Also the item is much lighter to lift about. If desired, economies can be made by using a matching simulated leather for the outside arms and outside back. Frequently the perfect match can be found, with a considerable saving in cost.

84 The first stuffing of a Chesterfield's arms and back.

85 The first stuffing of a Chesterfield's arm (closer view).

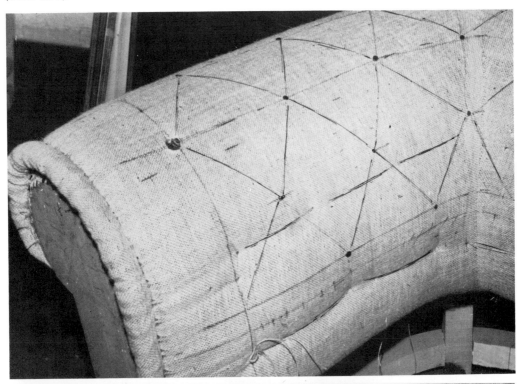

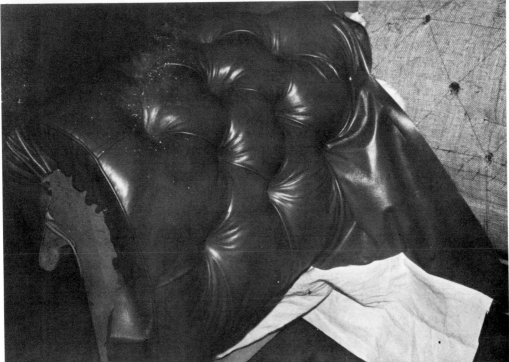

86 Arm of a Chesterfield in the process of being re-covered.

87 Covered arms and back of a Chesterfield.

SECTION SIX

Modern Materials and Methods

INTRODUCTION TO FOAM UPHOLSTERY

The modern materials which the upholsterer now has at his command have considerably reduced the skill needed to produce upholstered work and made it much easier for the learner to turn out a professional looking job. It is, however, still very necessary to exercise a great deal of care, thought and patience in carrying out the work to preserve that all important neat, tidy, tailored appearance. A great deal of success with upholstery is learning how to handle and manipulate materials, and this is gained only by practice. As with most craft work, it is advisable for the learner of upholstery to start with something comparatively simple, which needs no complicated shaping or cutting.

FOAM UPHOLSTERY OF STOOLS

We can take as first examples or exercises the two different types of stools shown in plates 88 and 89. Construction of the framework for these stools is simple, and very little woodworking knowledge, or experience in frame-making is needed. Upholstery of the stools is carried out with easy to work materials which can be obtained with little difficulty.

Two types of basic frame are used for these stools. One is a timber frame, using two side and two end members which are dowelled together. Metal plates are screwed to the underside at the corners to accommodate screw-in turned tapered legs (plate 88). The other is a piece of plywood, chipboard or blockboard cut to the size and shape of the base with cabriole legs.

The timber framed stool

This is an excellent example to use as an exercise for handicraft students, introducing different skills and producing a satisfying and useful end product. Materials used are shown in plate 90: seat frame, legs and plates, 3.8 cm ($1\frac{1}{2}$ in.) plastic foam, and rubber webbing. Some strips of calico or thin cotton material will also be needed, and covering material of a size sufficient to tack on the underside of the frame.

The size of the frame illustrated is 38 cm by 28 cm (15 in. by 11 in.). It is constructed from 4.8 cm by 2.2 cm ($1\frac{7}{8}$ in. by $\frac{7}{8}$ in.) beech timber; the dowelled joints have two 1 cm ($\frac{3}{8}$ in.) dowel pins at each joint. The addition of triangular corner blocks glued and screwed on the inside faces will give added strength to the frame. The joints must be cut absolutely square, and dowel holes and pins lined up accurately. After gluing and cramping, the frame should be left for 24 hours before any attempt is made at upholstery.

The first step in the upholstery work is the fixing of the webbing. Four single strands of 3.8 cm ($1\frac{1}{2}$ in.) wide rubber webbing are used, being attached only across the narrow width from each long side. Interlacing is not necessary as it would be with linen webbing. Tacks 1.2 cm ($\frac{1}{2}$ in.) in length should be used to attach the webbing to the frame. It is very important to hammer the tacks in straight so that their heads lie flat upon the webbing (figure 50 on page 73). Some difficulty may be experienced at first, and it would be wise to practice hammering tacks into a waste piece of timber to master this aspect of the work.

88 Simple stool upholstered with foam interior.

89 Period stool upholstered with foam.

From the illustration it is clear that a mis-placed tack could damage the webbing and weaken its holding power: in fact this is true of any material needing to be tacked, and must be remembered at all times.

Rubber webbing must be applied with varying degrees of tension depending on the area to be supported. In the case of this stool which has a fairly small area to be supported, little tension is required: approximately 2 cm ($\frac{3}{4}$ in.) will suffice. Plates 52 and 91 (on pages 74 and 144 respectively) illustrate two methods of tensioning the rubber webbing. It is possible to achieve the correct tension by hand straining, but if difficulty is found, a piece of wood the width of the webbing, and approximately 12.5 cm (5 in.) in length can be used as a lever. Plate 91 shows the method of wrapping the webbing around the timber to take the strain off the hands. Plate 51 on page 74 shows the method of marking the webbing at the inside line of the frame; this will enable the amount of elongation to be visible, and also will enable each strand to be tensioned alike which is essential.

Polyurethane or latex foam can be used for the interior padding. Polyurethane foam is more readily obtained, so we shall assume this will be the medium that most readers will be working with. A fairly firm density foam 3.8 cm ($1\frac{1}{2}$ in.) in thickness should be used, and cut fractionally oversize 0.3 cm ($\frac{1}{8}$ in.) larger than the framework. Plate 92 shows foam being cut with a sharp broad-bladed breadknife. This operation should be carried out carefully with long, firm strokes to obtain a straight upright edge. The knife should be used upright with the cutting line just over the edge of the sup-porting table.

After the cutting operation, a strip of calico or cotton fabric should be stuck approximately half way up the outer edges of the foam leaving a flange which will be tacked to the timber frame. There are several adhesives on the market suitable for plastics. The adhesive should be applied to both the surfaces to be put together. A spatula or broad bladed tool or knife can be used for this purpose (plate 93).

Plate 94 shows the flanges tacked to the frame using 1 cm ($\frac{3}{8}$ in.) tacks ready for the covering stage. The covering of the up-holstery is, of course, the most important stage. However well the interior has been constructed, covering applied badly will mar the appearance. Before attempting to place the covering in position centre marks should be put in the centres of the long edges (front and back edges) of the stool frame, and also on the covering: these should coincide when placing the covering in position. *Do not* attempt to tack the covering permanently straight away; temporary tacks (tacks partly hammered in) should be placed on the underside of the frame on all four sides to ensure that the fabric is placed straight, and that any pattern or the weave of the material is lined up with the sides or edges of the stool (plate 95).

Now that the covering is positioned with temporary tacks, and is perfectly straight, with the surface unwrinkled, we can proceed to permanently tack the fabric using 1 cm ($\frac{3}{8}$ in.) tacks. It is a great mistake to tack the material permanently too early in the operation. A little care and patience are amply rewarded with a more professional looking job.

The covering should not be strained too tightly, as this will reduce the height and distort the square appearance of the edge. A light tension with a smoothing action of the hand towards the corners is required, after the tacking has been started at the centres of the long sides. The material should be tacked to within 5 cm (2 in.) of the corner, leaving this so that the pleating can be manipulated. Corner pleating is left until all four sides have been tacked. Figure 27 on page 41 shows the two stages in the pleating. In stage one, the material is smoothed from the short side round to the front corner,

90 Frame and materials for simple stool with foam interior.

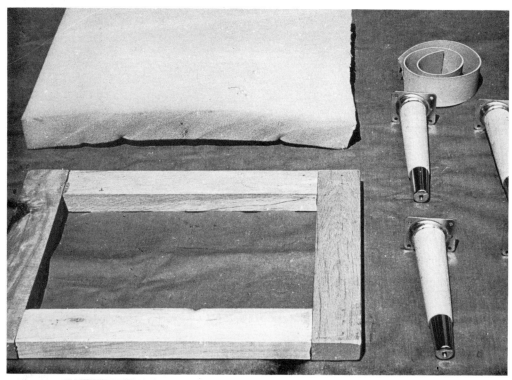

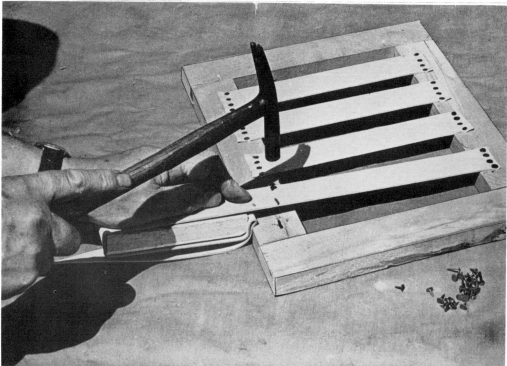

91 Tensioning rubber webbing with the aid of a block of timber.

92 Cutting foam with a broad-bladed knife.

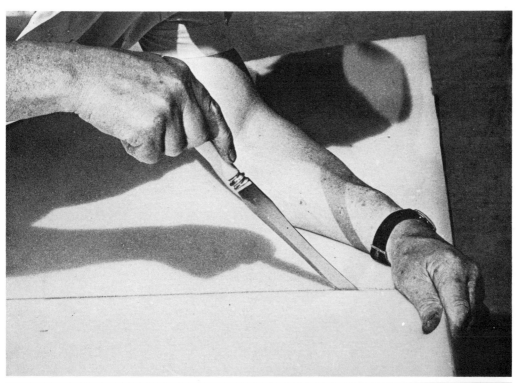

93 Applying adhesive to the edges of the foam
for the fixing flange.

94 Flanges tacked to frame to hold foam in position.

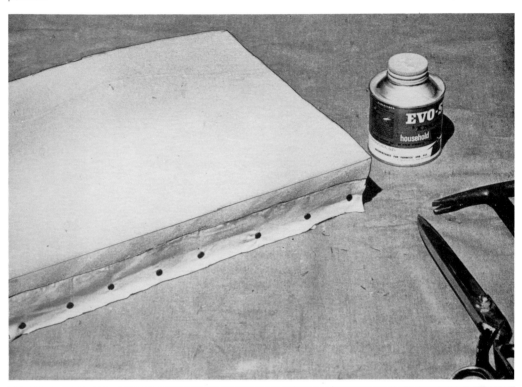

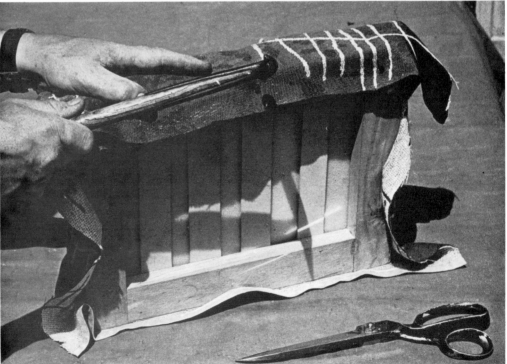

95 Covering being temporarily tacked in position on seat frame.

96 Fixing 'screw in' leg plates to the underside of stool frame.

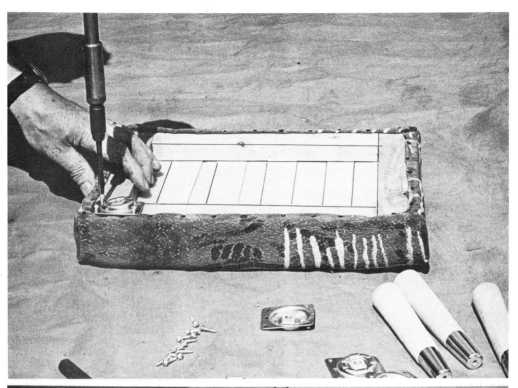

97 Materials for construction of Period style stool.

easing slightly downwards to remove any fullness at the top edge of the frame. In stage two the surplus material is cut away. This would be in a triangular shape, leaving sufficient material to fold under to form the pleat on the line of the corner of the frame and foam. The remainder of the covering can then continue to be tacked. The pleats can afterwards be slip-stitched if there is any tendency towards gaping.

To achieve a neat and tidy appearance to the underside, and to dispense with an undercover or bottom, the material should be folded under approximately 1.2 cm ($\frac{1}{2}$ in.) as it is being tacked. Particular attention should be paid to the corner pleats as they fold underneath the frame, to ensure there are no frayed ends or yarn protruding. The metal plates can now be screwed on to the corners of the frame, setting them if possible just inside the line of the tacked covering (plate 96).

The period style stool

Another method of making and upholstering a stool is by using a plywood, blockboard or chipboard base, cabriole legs and foam. Plate 97 shows a plywood base 45 cm by 45 cm (18 in. by 18 in.) in size, and 1.6 cm ($\frac{5}{8}$ in.) in thickness, 23 cm (9 in.) cabriole legs of beech and the foam for the filling. The completed upholstered height of this stool will be 32 cm (12$\frac{1}{2}$ in.) high.

After gathering the materials together, the first task is to glue and screw the legs in position, as this cannot be done after upholstery. It is advisable to mark the positions for the legs on the corners of the plywood, then use a template with the screw hole positions perforated on it, so that when they are marked through the holes will coincide exactly when drilled either by hand or electric drill. Three 5 cm (2 in.) by 7 gauge wood screws should be used in each leg. The legs should be glued in addition to screwing (plates 98 and 99).

The object of using three separate layers

of foam for this stool is to give the top surface a slightly domed effect usual with the traditional type of filling. This will give a more authentic appearance to our period piece. The two larger pieces of foam should be cut 0.6 cm ($\frac{1}{4}$ in.) larger all round than the size of the base. The third, smaller piece should be 7.5 cm (3 in.) smaller all round. Apply an adhesive suitable for plastics approximately 5 cm (2 in.) wide round the edges of one of the larger pieces of foam and ply. Take care when placing these together. Ensure that there is an equal slight overlap on the four sides.

Prepare the smaller piece by chamfering one edge (plate 100). The chamfer should have a fairly long slope of about 5 cm (2 in.). Adhesive is applied to this chamfered edge and also to the upper surface of the foam already stuck on the base. It is a help if the position on top of the chamfered insert, marked giving a guide to the adhesive application; this need be only from the extreme edge of the lower piece to the line of the inner edge of the chamfer. Apply the smaller foam insert with the chamfer to the underside (plate 101), pressing the edges well down, as the slight deformation of the foam will put a strain on the stuck chamfered edge. Now glue the third layer in position on top of the chamfered insert, taking care that the edges are flush and upright. The seat should now be nicely domed as shown in figures 88 and 89.

The stool is now ready for its final covering. This can be achieved in either of two ways. One is by applying the covering in one piece by means of the pull-over edge which is tacked to the underside of the plywood: plate 102 shows this method being carried out at the temporary tacking stage. The other, a more complicated method involving accurate cutting of the covering and machining, includes a ruched top edge (plate 89 on page 142). This is well worth the extra work if one is capable of machining or able to have the cover machined professionally.

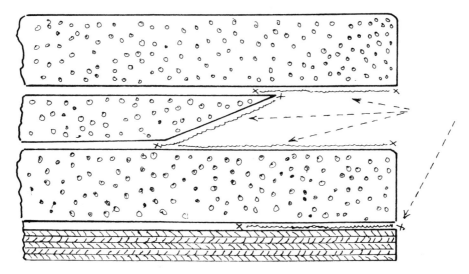

88 *Method of fabrication of foam.*

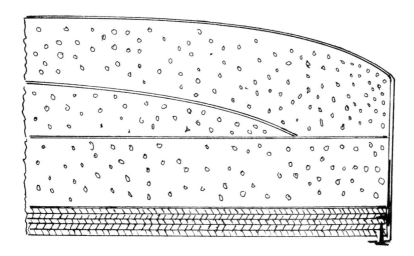

89 *The doming effect attained by laminating foam.*

98 Drilling plywood base ready for screwing of
the cabriole legs.

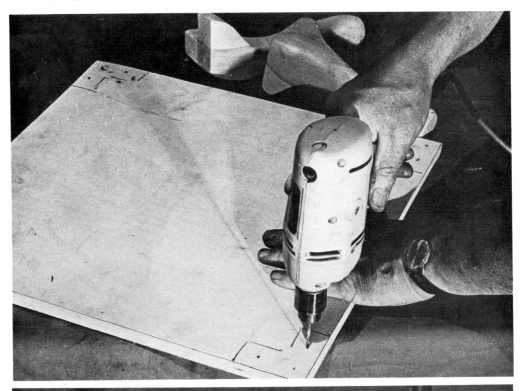

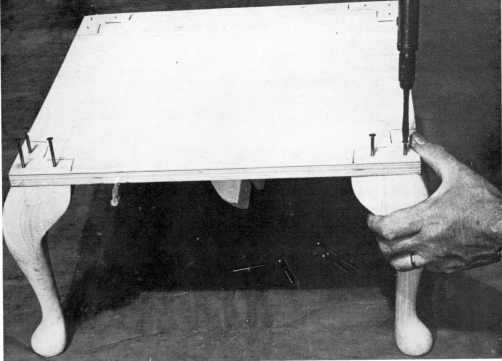

99 Screwing of cabriole legs to base plywood.

100 Chamfering edges of smaller doming piece of foam.

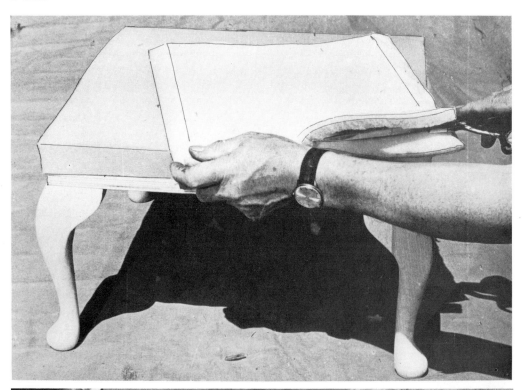

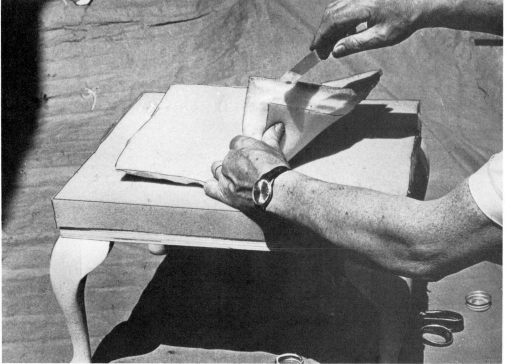

101 Applying adhesive to chamfered edge of small doming piece of foam.

If the first method is followed, make sure that the central motif of the covering is placed in the centre of the stool seat: as an aid to this, mark the centre of the framework before applying the covering. When the covering has been centred, and cleaned out of fullness and wrinkling, it can be tacked on the underside of the plywood base using 1 cm ($\frac{3}{8}$ in.) tacks. The corner pleats should be treated as shown in figure 27 on page 41, with the slight modification that the material should be tacked on the front or face edge of the plywood base where the legs are screwed at the corners. The fabric in this instance can be tacked singly, without folding it under at the corners or along the sides where it should be tacked to the underside. The raw edges of the fabric will be hidden by an undercover or bottom.

Having completely fixed the covering, now apply the undercovering or bottoming to give a neat and tidy appearance. This, of course, should be applied (as with all the materials we use) with the threads or weave running parallel with the sides. This is a principle one should always try to adopt as it is far easier to smooth, clean out, and tack materials which are straight than those which are on the skew (out of line with the edges of the frame).

Bottoming can be any form of a cheap plain cotton, linen or hessian which will give a neat appearance. The edges should be folded under approximately 1.2 cm ($\frac{1}{2}$ in.) and tacked about that distance from the outer edge of the frame, using 1 cm ($\frac{3}{8}$ in.) tacks placed approximately 4 cm to 5 cm ($1\frac{1}{2}$ in. to 2 in.) apart. Work on the four sides first. Cuts should then be made from the corners of the bottoming fabric to the projections of the innerside of the legs as shown in plate 103. This will enable the bottom to lay flat and unwrinkled when tacked.

The gimp, braid or fringe, which will hide any raw edges and tacks left visible, can be fixed with adhesive or be hand sewn.

Plate 104 shows adhesive being applied to a braid. The adhesive can be either a tube glue, such as seccotine or Uhu, or a type such as Copydex which is recommended for carpet binding, etc. This can be obtained in bottle form with a brush supplied ideal for applying to the braid. Adhesive should be applied sparingly, using a small brush, spatula, or flat-bladed instrument. Care should be taken not to overrun the edges of the braid. Only one surface need be coated as these adhesives are not the contact type. After applying the adhesive along a stretch of about 15 cm to 20 cm (6 in. to 8 in.) the braid should be pressed firmly to the covering, and a few 'temporary' tacks placed at intervals along the braid to hold it in position until the adhesive has set. These can easily be removed later. Do avoid hammering tacks permanently into the braid so that they are plainly visible, this always mars the final appearance.

The second method of dealing with the top covering is a more ambitious project for the beginner, but for anyone with experience of soft furnishing, or useful with the sewing machine, it should present little difficulty. The basic frame and foam filling is made up as for the pull-over edge. Once this has been constructed, cutting sizes can be established. As mentioned earlier, the foam filling should be slightly oversize. This is to ensure that a slight tension is given to the covering by the compression of the foam to the frame size. Also it must be appreciated that the distance across the centre domed section is greater than that along the straight edges. This must be allowed for in the cutting of the top panel.

Mark out (preferably with tailor's chalk on the reverse side of the fabric) the top panel to the size of the frame plus 1 cm ($\frac{3}{8}$ in.) for seaming on each edge. In addition to this, to accommodate the doming at the centre of the seat, allow an extra 0.6 cm ($\frac{1}{4}$ in.) at the centres of all sides gradually diminishing to the normal seaming size at the corners (figure 90). Four borders should be cut the same length as the sides of the top panel, the depth of the borders being the total height of the upholstery plus the allowance for seaming on the top edge and approximately 2 cm ($\frac{3}{4}$ in.) for tacking to the underside of the frame. The borders should be joined at the corners with the ruching sewn into the top seams only. It is essential that if the material be patterned or striped, as the example illustrated, care should be taken in matching. Finishing of the stool is as previously described.

90 *Cutting of top panel for ruched stool.*

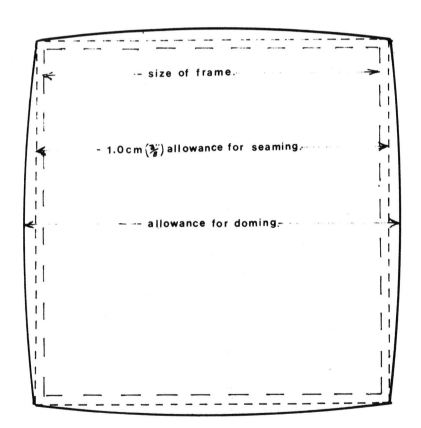

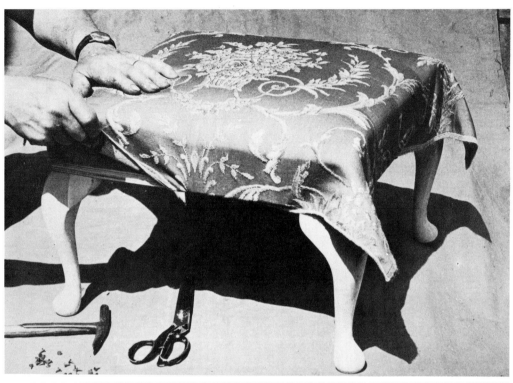

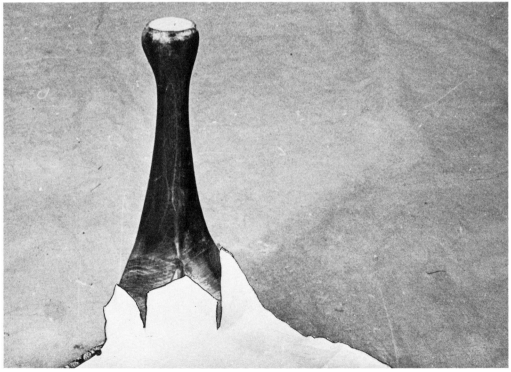

102 The 'pull-over' finish to the edge of the stool.

103 Cutting of bottoming round base of cabriole leg.

104 Applying adhesive to the gimp or braid.

The circular stool

Plate 105 shows components for a circular stool. Two strips of 0.6 cm ($\frac{1}{4}$ in.) foam which, joined together, will girdle the circumference, are included here. It will be found that the edges of a chipboard or blockboard circle, when cut by hand, will tend to be ragged. By sticking the two thin layers of foam round the circumference, a better and smoother edge will be obtained. The circular stool can be finished on the top edge with a plain or ruched seam. The upholstery construction will be similar to that of the period style stool described above.

105 Materials for circular stool – to be finished
as Plate 89.

UPHOLSTERY OF HEADBOARDS USING FOAM

The earlier buttoned bed headboards and footboards were usually upholstered in the traditional manner with an interior filling of horsehair and wadding applied to a framed-up construction. Hessian and webbing lined the frame to support the filling. Generally, the restoration of this type of traditionally upholstered headboard will necessitate the complete removal of all the materials from the frame to enable the hessian and webbing to be replaced. Often the webbing and hessian will have become over-stretched or have deteriorated to an unusable degree. There is normally no first stuffing and stitching to carry out on a headboard. After replacing the hessian and webbing, re-marking the button positions if buttoned, teasing and replacing the fillings with wadding over, the upholstery can then be covered and buttoned. The covering fabric, or a cheaper substitute, can be used for the reverse side of the headboard.

The modern counterparts of the deep buttoned bed headboard are as popular as ever, giving a touch of class to my lady's bed chamber. Moreover, they are much simpler in construction, and easier both to restore and to make from scratch. Plywood, chipboard or laminated board may be used as the basis of the headboard. The cheapest of these materials is chipboard. Sheet foam can be used for the filling. If the original headboard is of un-upholstered polished timber, this can be used as a backboard for the upholstery if desired.

The first step in the making of the headboard is to decide on its shape and style. It can be either a modern rectangular plainly upholstered one, or a more elaborate, curved Queen Anne style. The board itself is most easily and quickly cut on a machine band

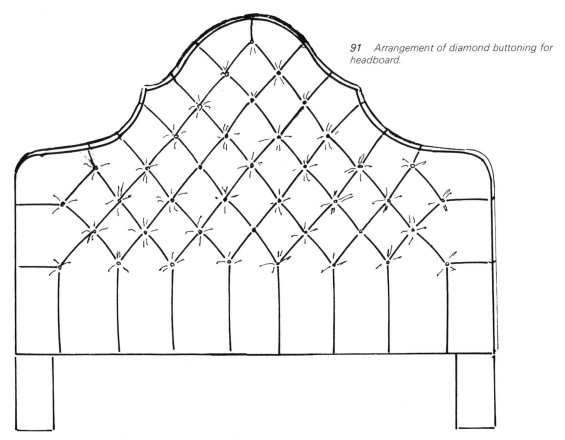

91 Arrangement of diamond buttoning for headboard.

saw, but can, if necessary, be cut with a bow or pad saw. Care must be taken to ensure that the shapes are identical on both sides. It is advisable to work from a template marking one side and then reversing the template for the other side. Any rough edges or sharp points left after the sawing should be removed by sanding with glasspaper.

Either urethane or latex foam should be cut to the shape of the backboard, but fractionally oversize (plate 106). Foam 3.6 cm (1½ in.) thick and of medium firm density will normally be suitable. Once the positions of the buttons have been decided on, 1.2 cm (½ in.) holes should be cut right through the foam from one side to the other. The holes can easily be made with a piece of metal tube of the same diameter. File the end of the tube to make a cutting edge which can then be hammered through the foam on to a firm wooden base. Use a piece of timber, not stone or iron, as the latter will ruin

the cutting edge of the tube after one or two holes have been made. A suitable arrangement for the buttons is shown in plate 106 where the foam has been prepared for sticking on to the baseboard. It is only necessary to apply adhesive to the area around the outsides of the button positions. No adhesive is needed in the central area.

A choice can be made between the use of normal upholstery buttons or button studs. The normal upholstery button will have a fabric tuft or wire loop on the reverse side, whilst the stud will have a tack protruding from the inside of the button so that it may be hammered into position into the timber base. These buttons and studs are shown in figure 72 on page 101. Either type can be made up by the professional button maker using fabric supplied. Alternatively, a form of wire loop button can be made by using D.I.Y. button components. Whilst these are suitable for buttoning headboards where there is only a limited amount of strain on the button loops they are not suitable for the deep buttoning of chair and settee seats and backs.

If it is decided to use buttons with wire loops or tufts, holes should be drilled through the timber base to allow the twine which is to hold each button to pass through to the back, and be fixed. A 0.6 cm ($\frac{1}{4}$ in.) hole would be of suitable size. A smaller size makes it difficult to locate and pass the needle through. The holes in the timber should match up with the holes made on the foam. The size of the diamonds or distance between the buttons should never be too close, probably not less than 12.5 cm (5 in.), as this would result in too many buttons and create a rather over-powering effect. A suitable arrangement is shown in figure 91.

An earlier chapter (see page 99) mentions the amount of fullness that should be allowed for deep diamond buttoning on traditional seating and backs. It should be remembered that in this case foam of only 3.6 cm ($1\frac{1}{2}$ in.) thickness is being used, and this will not result in such a deep indentation as hair filling would. Consequently, it will not be necessary to allow quite so much fullness when marking the button positions on the covering. It is advisable to test the measurement after marking by pulling a tape measure over the foam between the holes to obtain a depth of indentation consistent with the size of diamond and firmness of the foam.

Once the covering has been marked on the reverse side, the twine should be threaded through the back tuft or loop of the button, and then passed through the appropriate marks in the covering, and thence through the holes in the foam and the baseboard. Temporary tacks should be put at the side of the holes on the back of the board and the twine caught on to these with slip knots which should be gently eased down one after the other whilst the pleats between the buttons are smoothed into position with the flat end of a regulator. Before completing the tying off of the buttons, the covering should be temporarily tacked and cleaned out along the tops and sides, then tacked home. Finish off by tacking home the twine ties. It will be noted that in the case of the buttoning of the headboard, the buttons are being inserted from the face of the work to the back, and tacked off, whereas with the normal deep button work, the buttons are best tied off on the face.

If button studs are to be used instead of tufted or wire loop buttons, it is unnecessary to drill holes in the timber base. Positions for the studs should be clearly marked so that when inserting the studs the marks may be seen through the holes in the foam. The button studs must be hammered home carefully to avoid damaging the covering fabric, and they must be hammered in squarely without tilting, so that the button sits flat. This method is not advisable when using velvet as the hammer will mark the velvet.

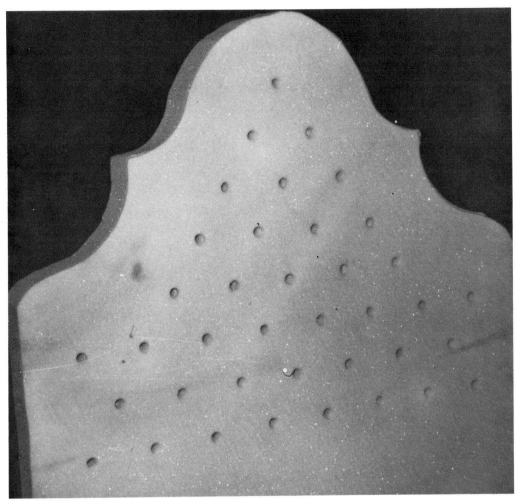

106 Foam cut and drilled to take buttons for buttoned headboard.

UPHOLSTERY RESTORATION COVERING

Period	Frame constructions	Typical motifs of period	Typical coverings used
Early Jacobean	Simple turned legs Square constructions Oak timber	Oak leaf branches Fruit and flowers Vase and pineapple	Italian velvets Leather Linen Tapestry (*petit point* and *gross point* work)
Cromwellian	Heavy oak Dark finish Turning and carving on backs	As above	Mainly leather brass studded
Late Jacobean	Lighter and more elaborate turning on legs Walnut timber	Acanthus leaf Flowers Birds	Cane Velvets Silk Tapestries Damasks Elaborate trimmings
William and Mary	More delicate constructions with high backs Shaped and carved legs Walnut timber Some gilt	Formal flowers (replicas of Dutch flower paintings) and motifs similar to Jacobean	Indian printed cotton (chintz) Leather *Petit point* work Damasks Brocades Crewel work Rush
Queen Anne	Carved walnut cabriole Claw and ball feet More sober designs Less ornamentation	Scallop shells Acanthus leaves Flowers, more natural and delicate than Jacobean	First use of stuffover upholstery Rush Leather Wool or silk needlework (influenced by designs of oriental carpets)

Chippendale	Mahogany timber Easy chairs with low backs and wide seats Ribbon carving Some Chinese styles	Detached sprigs of flowers, Ribbons Knots Cupid's bows Garlands Medallions	French brocades Floral *petit point* Satins Genoa velvets Plush Geometrical wool work Tapestry or needlework Panel designs on plain grounds
Adam	Light classical styles Some gilt finishes French styles	Classical urns Wreaths Knots Rams' or goats' heads Lozenges Honeysuckle Medallions Draped figures	Damasks Tapestry Leather
Hepplewhite	Delicate and elegant styles Carved mahogany and painted beechwood, satinwood	Wheat ears Ferns Prince of Wales' feathers Loops of drapery	Striped satin Silks Damasks Red or blue morocco Medallion designs on silk
Sheraton	Feminine styles Curved backs Japanned and painted beechwood	Inlaid shells Flower swags Vases Lyres and other classical motifs	Finely drawn designs on floral chintz Striped or flowered satins and brocades Black horsehair covering Occasional cane
Regency	Classical styles Light constructions Various woods Brass ornamentation	Classical wreaths Floral swags Festoons Urns Vases	Striped satin Damasks Brocades Velvets

GLOSSARY

Back-tacking Method of attaching covering to conceal tacking on outside backs and arms with straight edges.

Bias cutting Cutting fabric diagonally across threads.

Bible front A bold rounded edge to front of seat.

Blind stitch Stitches formed with twine to consolidate filling.

Bottoming A muslin cover tacked to the underside.

Bridle ties Loops of twine to hold filling in place.

Burlap *see* Hessian.

Buttoning Method of forming deep diamond shapes with carefully positioned buttons.

Calico White muslin (fine cotton) material, available in a variety of weights, used for undercovering or bottoming.

Chamfer An edge that is shaved or rounded, required when making a bevel on a corner of timber, or joining two welts of leather.

Chipboard Heavy-duty cardboard used as backing in low-stress areas such as headboards, or as tacking strips.

Coil springs Steel wire spirals, available in various sizes and wire gauges.

Collar Strip of material fitted round shaped cuts (e.g. show-wood arms) to prevent gaping when stiles are cut.

Cored foam Foam made with openings on one side. The weight and resiliency is determined by thickness, and by diameter of cores. For reversible cushions, two pieces are glued together with cored sides facing.

Cotton wadding Cotton felt used to cover loose fillings to create a smooth surface. Available in rolls or by the yard; thickness is determined by weight per yard.

Deck Area under a removable cushion on a sprung seat. A sturdy coordinating fabric is machined to top covering just past the well to cover this concealed area.

Doming Degree of rise in centre of seat or cushion.

Double cone spring Spring with large top and bottom coil and narrow waist.

Dowels Grooved wooden pegs glued into predrilled holes to form furniture frame joints.

Drop-in seat A loose seat to fit into rebate of dining chair or bedroom stool.

Dust cover *see* Bottoming

Fibre filling Loose stuffing used to soften and shape the spring and frame edges.

Fillets Additional small pieces of timber added to frame.

Float buttoning Buttons lightly pulled into covering.

Flys Extension pieces of hessian etc, machine stitched to final cover where they will not be seen, to economize with covering.

Fullness Surplus covering causing wrinkling.

Gauge Thickness of wire used to make spiral springs, the lowest number representing the thickest wire and the highest number the finest.

Gimp Narrow woven tape used to cover tacks and raw edges on show-wood furniture; available in a variety of textures and colours, also used for decoration.

Gimp pins Fine tacks with rounded heads to hold gimp in place; virtually invisible in use.

Glasspaper Sandpaper used to smooth rough edges on furniture frames, and to clean excess glue from joints.

Gutter A channel formed in hessian for spring edge (*see* Well).

Hessian A rough woven jute cloth, also known as burlap.

Join A machine-stitched seam used to connect two pieces of fabric.

K.D. (Knock down) Furniture made in separate parts for ease of transport.

Laidcord Heavy cord made from flax or hemp fibre for lashing springs. 'Laid' refers to the method of manufacture, which makes the cord stretch-resistant.

Lashing The lacing and knotting together of spring coils with heavy twine to prevent lateral movement.

Laminated webbing Rubber webbing with rayon threads within layers of rubber.

Lead moulding Trimming for leather upholstery to hide tacks or gimp pins.

Lip Front edge of cushion seat.

Mock cushion Construction of seat to imitate a cushion.

Mortice, mortise Hole cut into timber to accommodate a tenon (projection) to form a mortice and tenon joint.

Picking Separating and fluffing up hard-packed portions of fibre stuffing by hand or machine.

Pin-stuffed An upholstery seat using one layer of filling only.

Pincers Pliers used to extract small tacks and staples from furniture frames.

Platform Rear surface of cushion seat.

Plywood gusset A triangular piece of plywood used to strengthen joints.

Pull-over edge A seat front edge with covering 'pulled' straight over.

Rebate A recess or groove cut near the edge of the frame to support a drop-in seat or to provide a tacking area.

Refurbishing Repairing or renewing.

Ripping Stripping of covering or filling from frame.

Roll edge A roll edge prevents stuffing from working away from the edge of the frame. Commercially made rolls can be purchased by the yard.

Ruche Decorative trimming to hide join in covering.

Sash cramp A bar or pipe clamp used when regluing loose joints.

Scrim Open or loosely woven fabric made from flax yarn.

Serpentine spring Continuous wire spring formed from zigzag strip, requiring no webbing.

Show-wood chair An upholstered frame with polished wood showing.

Silencer Strip of webbing or sturdy material placed between the unfastened spring coils and frame to prevent rattling when the depressed springs hit the wood.

Single cone spring Spring with large top coil with seat tapering to base.

Sinuous spring *see* Serpentine spring.

Skewers Long upholsterers' pins with ring at one end.

Skivering Shaving the underside of leather to reduce thickness.

Spring edge A flexible edge for seats or backs.

Squab Flat firmly-stuffed cushion.

Stile Part of frame construction around which covering must be cut.

Stitched edge A padded edge formed over the front of the spring burlap to create the desired finished shape.

Stuffover chair Chair completely stuffed over and covered.

Tack roll Method of making a soft edge on a timber frame.

Tack ties Lines caused in covering through faulty tacking.

Tacking strips Narrow chipboard strips used to reinforce tacked final covering edges.

Tension spring Elongated expanding spring for seats and backs.

Top stuffed Interior upholstery applied to top surface of seat members only and not within the frame.

Trestles Saw horses built with padded tops with raised edges so that furniture will not slip off or be scratched.

Under the edge Forming an overlapping roll on the front of the seat.

Unit spring An assembly of springs to fit a seat or back.

Vandyking Method of joining covering for diamond buttoning.

Warp Threads running down length of fabric, parallel to selvedge.

Webbing Strips woven from jute fibre to provide support for filling materials.

Weft Threads running across width of fabric.

Well A depression formed behind the first row of springs in a lashed spring seat.

Welt A cord covered with diagonally cut strips of covering or contrasting fabric; also commercially made.

LIST OF SUPPLIERS

Great Britain

WHOLESALE SUPPLIERS FOR THE PROFESSIONAL AND EDUCATIONAL MARKETS (MAIL AND NATIONAL CARRIER DELIVERY SERVICE)

A.C. Freeman & Sons Ltd
Cromwell Road, Boscombe,
Bournemouth, Hants BH5 2JW

M. Donaldson Ltd
4/8 Temperance Street,
Torquay, Devon TQ2 5PX

C.K. Supplies
Ground Floor, Stubbs Mill, 1 Percy Street,
Ancoats, Manchester 4

D.L. Forster
17 Tramway Avenue, Stratford,
London E15 4PG

Glover Brothers
5 Redchurch Street, Shoreditch,
London E2

Jacksons (Upholsterers Supplies Ltd)
368 Argyle Street, Glasgow C2

James John & Sons
Studley, Warwickshire

Poulton & Nicholson
98 Curtain Road, Shoreditch, London E2

J.H. Porter
Portland House, Norlington Road,
Leyton, London E10

J. Singleton Ltd
Red Bank, North Street,
Manchester M8 8QF

RETAIL OUTLET FOR THE AMATEUR MARKET

D.L. Forster, 17 Tramway Avenue,
Stratford, London E15 4PG

Upon receipt of letter this establishment
will forward details of local distributors of
upholstery sundries for the amateur.
Supplying basic tools, upholstery tacks,
cut lengths of hessian, calico, lining,
rubber webbing and clips, Dacron filling,
crumbled foam, etc.

U.S.A.

Some of the firms listed below may sell only wholesale or in bulk quantities. Request the name of a distributor in your area. For an alternate source of the needed supplies contact a local upholsterer who can probably sell you what you need.

FABRIC

Crompton-Richmond Co., Inc.
1071 Avenue of the Americas, New York, N.Y. 10018

Ford Motor Co.
Chemical Products Div., 3001 T Miller Rd., Dearborn, Mich. 48120

F. Schumacher & Co.
939 Third Ave., New York, N.Y. 10022

J.P. Stevens & Co.
1185 Avenue of the Americas, New York, N.Y. 10036

FIBER

Blocksom & Co.
406 Center St., Michigan City, Ind. 46360

Duracote Corp.
358 N. Diamond St., Ravenna, Ohio 44266

Excelsior, Inc.
726 Chestnut St., Rockford, Ill. 61102

International Textile, Inc.
2610 N. Pulaski Rd., Chicago, Ill. 60639

Universal Fibres, Inc.
65 9 St., Brooklyn, N.Y. 11215

FOAM

Accurate Foam Co.
819 Fox St., La Porte, Ind. 46350

Fairmont Corp.
625 N. Michigan Ave., Chicago, Ill. 60611

Firestone Foam Products Co.
823 Waterman Ave., P.O. Box 4159, E. Providence, R.I. 02914

Foamage, Inc.
506 S. Garland, Orlando, Fla. 32801

Perma Foam, Inc.
605-R 21 St., Irvington, N.J. 07111

SPRINGS

Barber Mfg. Co., Inc.
1824 Brown St., P.O. Box 2454, Anderson, Ind. 46016

Dudek & Bock Spring Mfg. Co.
5102 W. Roosevelt Rd., Chicago, Ill. 60650

Select-A-Spring Corp.
190 Railroad Ave., Jersey City, N.J. 07302

Starcraft Mfg. Co.
16918 Edwards Rd., Cerritos, Calif. 90701

LIST OF ADDRESSES

ASSOCIATIONS AND SOCIETIES

Association of Master Upholsterers (AMU)
Dormar House, Mitre Ridge,
Scrubbs Lane, London NW10

British Furniture Manufacturers Federated Associations (BFM)
17 Berners Street, London W1P 4DY

British Standards Institute (BSI)
2 Park Street, London W1A 2BS

City and Guilds of London Institute
76 Portland Place, London W1N 4AA

The Design Centre
28 Haymarket, London SW1Y 4SU

Furniture Industry Research Association (FIRA)
Maxwell Road, Stevenage, Herts

Furniture and Timber Industry Training Board (FTITB)
31 Octagon Parade, High Wycombe, Bucks

Furniture and Timber & Allied Trades Union (FTAT)
Fairfields, Roe Green, Kingsbury, London NW9 0PT

London and South Eastern Furniture Manufacturers Association (LFM)
93 Great Eastern Street, London EC2A 3JE

Scottish Furniture Manufacturers Association
Gordon Chambers, 90 Mitchell Street, Glasgow C1

Worshipful Company of Furniture Makers
c/o John Ward & Co, Robertsbridge, Sussex

Society of Designer Craftsmen
6 Queen Square, London WC2

COLLEGES

The following colleges offer courses in furniture making including upholstery. Where demand exists some offer Part-time classes.

St Albans: College of Building
Birmingham: Polytechnic
Brighton: Polytechnic
Bristol: Brunel Technical College
Bridgend: Technical College
Burnley: Technical College
Cambridge: College of Arts and Technology
Edinburgh: Telford College
Glasgow: College of Building & Printing
Huddersfield: Technical College
Hull: Technical College
High Wycombe: College of Art and Technology
Ipswich: Civic College
Kirkcaldy: Technical College
Leicester: Southfields College
Liverpool: College of Further Education
Leeds: Jacob Kramer
London: College of Furniture
Manchester: College of Building
Norwich: City College
Nottingham: Basford Hall
Newcastle: College of Arts and Technology
Portsmouth: Highbury College
Sheffield: Shirecliffe College
Southend: College of Technology
Sunderland: Wearsdale College of Further Education
Tottenham: Technical College
West Bromwich: College of Technology
Wisbech: Isle of Ely College of Further Education

INDEX